D0111368

WITHDRAWN
University of
Illinois Library
at Urbana-Champaign

SWING THAT MUSIC

NOTICE: Return or renew all Library Materials! The *Minimum* Fee for
each Lost Book is $50.00.

The person charging this material is responsible for
its return to the library from which it was withdrawn
on or before the **Latest Date** stamped below.

**Theft, mutilation, and underlining of books are reasons for discipli-
nary action and may result in dismissal from the University.**
To renew call Telephone Center, 333-8400

UNIVERSITY OF ILLINOIS LIBRARY AT URBANA-CHAMPAIGN

JAN 07 2000
VMB 3/19/07

MAR 1 3 2004

4/30/07

11/29/18

L161—O-1096

Copyright The Conde Nast Publications, Inc.

LOUIS ARMSTRONG

SWING THAT MUSIC

BY

LOUIS ARMSTRONG

WITH AN INTRODUCTION BY
RUDY VALLEE
AND A NEW FOREWORD BY
DAN MORGENSTERN

MUSIC SECTION

EDITED BY
HORACE GERLACH

WITH SPECIAL EXAMPLES OF SWING MUSIC
CONTRIBUTED BY
BENNY GOODMAN — TOMMY DORSEY — JOE VENUTI
LOUIS ARMSTRONG — BUD FREEMAN — RED NORVO
CLAUDE HOPKINS — CARL KRESS — STANLEY DENNIS
RAY BAUDUC

DA CAPO PRESS • NEW YORK

Library of Congress Cataloging-in-Publication Data

Swing that music / by Louis Armstrong ; with an introduction by Rudy
   Vallee and a new foreword by Dan Morgenstern ; music section edited
   by Horace Gerlach ; with special examples of swing music contributed
   by Benny Goodman ... [et al.].
        p.   cm.
   Originally published: London ; New York : Longmans, Green,
1936. With new foreword.
   ISBN 0-306-80544-8
   1. Jazz--History and criticism. 2. Armstrong, Louis, 1900-1971.
3. Jazz musicians--United States--Biography.   I. Vallee, Rudy,
1901-   . II. Morgenstern, Dan. III. Gerlach, Horace.
IV. Goodman, Benny, 1909-   .
ML3506.S95   1993
781.65'09--dc20   93-21594
                                                      CIP
                                                       MN

First Da Capo Press edition 1993

This Da Capo Press paperback edition of *Swing That Music* is an
unabridged republication of the edition published in New York in
1936, with the addition of a new foreword by Dan Morgenstern.
It is reprinted by arrangement with The Louis Armstrong
Educational Foundation, Inc.

Copyright © 1936 by Louis Armstrong
Copyright renewed 1964 in the name of Louis Armstrong
Foreword copyright © 1993 by Dan Morgenstern

Published by Da Capo Press, Inc.
A Subsidiary of Plenum Publishing Corporation
233 Spring Street, New York, N.Y. 10013

All Rights Reserved

Manufactured in the United States of America

ML 3506   music
A 7559

INSCRIPTION

To the memory of the original "Dixieland Five," to "King" Oliver, to "Bix" Beiderbecke and Eddie Lang, now gone, and those other pioneers of a quarter of a century past, known and unknown, who created and carried to the world a native American music, who created Swing. And, finally, to the young musicians of today who will carry it on.

LOUIS ARMSTRONG

FOREWORD TO THE
DA CAPO EDITION

A more fitting subject than Louis Armstrong could not be imagined for the first published biography of a jazz musician. However, *Swing That Music* (out of print for some 55 years, astonishingly) is not only biography, but also one of the earliest American attempts to trace the development of jazz—then thought to be a music that had just culminated in something called "Swing."

It could well be said that Armstrong spent a lifetime working on his autobiography. From his earliest surviving letters (1922) to his last known jottings (1970), he spun out tales that add up to fascinating variations on a theme. This, his first published writing, is not always in his own true voice. But enough of it is to make the book more than a historical curiosity.

In 1936 (the official publication date of *Swing That Music* was November 7), precious little was known about jazz history. Marshall Stearns, then a graduate student at Yale, had begun to contribute a serialized history to *Down Beat*, the two-year-old periodical for dance band musicians. The revised English-language version of Hugues Panassie's *Le Jazz Hot*, called *Hot Jazz*, had been published a few months prior to Armstrong's book, but it was a guide to jazz appreciation and esthetics focusing on phonograph records, rather than a history. Robert Goffin's 1932 *Aux Frontiers du Jazz* was not translated. (It was, not so incidentally, dedicated to Louis Armstrong.) Such earlier works as Henry Osgood's *So This is Jazz* dealt with the peppy dance the term stood for in the "jazz age" rather than the African-American idiom of which a small but growing number of devotees had gradually become aware by 1936.

It is worth noting that *Swing That Music* pays tribute to the so-called Hot Clubs of Europe and contains a healthy plug for their newly-founded U.S. counterparts, which never really got off the ground—with the exception of the Chicago Hot Club, under first Helen Oakley, then Squirrel Ashcraft. During Armstrong's two stays in Europe, especially the much longer second one (from July 1933 to January 1935), he had become aware of the importance to the music of record collectors, budding critics and discographers, and other serious jazz fans. Throughout his life he would show extraordinary tolerance for this odd and often irritating breed.

Speaking of discography, in 1936 two other pioneering works were published, in London and Paris respectively: Hilton Schleman's *Rhythm On Record* and Charles Delauney's *Hot Discography*. Slowly but surely, tools were beginning to appear with which a listener could grope through the not-so-dim yet murky past of what clearly was a music to reckon with. *Swing That Music* was such a tool.

In retrospect, the history this book provides is slight, and its emphasis on the so-called "Dixieland Five," better known today as the Original Dixieland Jazz Band, seems, shall we say, politically incorrect. In this regard, we should remember that 1936 was also the year in which the four surviving members of the ODJB were reunited with considerable publicity and, perhaps even more significantly, that in his second book, *Satchmo: My Life in New Orleans* (Da Capo Press), first published in 1954, Armstrong mentions having bought the ODJB's records, including "the first *Tiger Rag* to be recorded. (Between you and me, it's still the best.)"

Of considerable significance was what Armstrong wrote about King Oliver and other New Orleans pioneers—Buddy Bolden, Freddy (sic) Keppard, Emmanuel Perez, Kid Ory, Big Eye Louis (Nelson) and Buddy Peete—a garbling of "Petit." There is much about Fate Marable and the riverboat bands, and such facts (dimly known at the time) as the personnel of King Oliver's Creole Jazz Band when Armstrong joined it.

Most interesting, of course, is what Armstrong has to say about his own life and experiences. Here, the broad outlines largely agree with his later and more detailed accounts, as in *Satchmo*. But there are things that do not quite add up, and a few that clearly seem wrong, such as the statement that the 1929 trip from Chicago to New York by the entire Carrol Dickerson band was their own idea, when we know that Armstrong had been invited and the others rode in on his agreeable coattails. The closer we come to 1936, the more sketchy the facts. There is even precious little about the first New York stay with Fletcher Henderson's band.

On the other hand, nowhere else does Armstrong give so detailed an account of the riverboat's itinerary or of daily life on board. The melodramatic tale of the wedding and its tragic aftermath seems invented; in *Satchmo*, the sole incident involving a passenger going overboard is a prank. The lengthy business about the ship's captain who knew Mark Twain, and Armstrong's supposed interest in this great writer, seems a bit suspect since it is never mentioned in his later autobiographical writings or interviews. One is left with the hunch that it was the ghostwriter or editor (who may have been one and the same) who had read *Tom Sawyer*, not Armstrong (though he certainly might have), and who thought that any account of life on the Mississippi should include Twain. Furthermore, the style of this portion of the book is clearly influenced by Twain's Sawyer-Huck Finn voice.

But the tale of how Armstrong, Marable, and Davey Jones mesmerized the St. Louis musicians who'd invited them to play rings true, though told only here. The pace of the earlier part of the biography indicates that it was based on Armstrong's own written or dictated materials, while the later passages more likely were adapted from interview notes. As is so often the case with book projects, time may simply have run out—or someone decided that the manuscript was getting too long.

Who was the ghost? Was it Horace Gerlach, who is the acknowledged editor of the scant ten pages so grandly headed "Part Two: Music Section" and co-composer and lyricist of the title tune so grandly presented as end matter? The music section is such gibberish—"arrant nonsense," in the opinion of *Melody Maker*'s Dan Ingman, in the most detailed contemporary review I was able to find—that one doubts that Mr. Gerlach was sufficiently competent to bring the ghosting off. What is one to think of a musician-writer who renders *Vesti La Giubba* as *Vesta Laqubla* and introduces us to "Sampson" and Delilah? (Or of an editor who let such things come to print?)

After considerable digging in the Institute of Jazz Studies' archives with help from ASCAP's Karen Sherry and Joe Muranyi, the clarinetist in the last Armstrong All Stars, we have found out a thing or two about Horace Gerlach. He was born in 1909 and died in 1984. We have as yet no proof of his claim that he arranged for Armstrong's big band. Aside from the tune that gave this book its title, he also co-wrote with Armstrong the songs "If We Never Meet Again," "Heart Full Of Rhythm," and "What Is This Thing Called Swing." After this last title from 1939, he disappears from the trumpeter's circle. With Bobby Burke, he wrote a 1949 hit by the Mills Brothers, "Daddy's Little Girl," and he later collaborated with William (Billy) Krechmer—who for years ran a bar in Philadelphia that was a favorite hangout for jazz musicians—on a couple of obscure songs. Aside from Armstrong, Gerlach's best-known collaborator was Jimmy Van Heusen, with whom he did "Love In the Air." Gerlach worked as intermission pianist at Jimmy Ryan's on 52nd Street in the club's early years. In a letter to Muranyi, he insisted that he was the sole author of this book's title tunc. That may be so; it would not be the first instance of a famous band leader getting his name on a copyright, though it seems unlike the Armstrong we knew. On the other hand, a man capable of writing (about Armstrong's trumpet playing) that "by skipping up or down in natural sequence, from one note to the next in position, he produces concordant melody" is not to be trusted! Don't get me wrong; Gerlach undoubtedly meant well, and in 1936 he was only 25, clearly caught up in the budding Swing craze of which this book was a product.

Armstrong's cause is better served by Rudy Vallee's introduction. Though not a likely choice for such a task, the noted crooner comes through with flying colors, in particular when he addresses Armstrong's singing. Moreover, Vallee wasn't all talk when it came to championing Armstrong. In 1937 he arranged for a real breakthrough in network radio when he persuaded his sponsor, Fleischman's Yeast, to engage Armstrong and his band for a series of commercial shows in what would now be called prime time.

Like this book, that was an Armstrong "first" for his race, and for the music he not merely represented but incarnated. Just slightly past the half-way mark of his remarkable life, Louis Armstrong would continue to swing that music and break down cultural and social barriers for years to come. It's good to have this rare memento back in circulation.

—DAN MORGENSTERN
May, 1993

A note on the solo transcriptions: In all probability, the ten musicians invited to contribute had their solo chorus captured by a recording device, perhaps with Gerlach as the pianist (the notated piano parts are in any case identical). The transcriptions are rather elementary, with no dynamic markings and few other interpretative aids. As for the musicians chosen, the fact that only Armstrong and Claude Hopkins were African-American is a sign of the times; on the other hand, the eight white players were certainly big names and, with the exception of Stanley Dennis, then with the very popular Casa Loma Orchestra, should be familiar to the reader. It's safe to say that no other popular song ever got such a sendoff, and while it never became a big hit, "Swing That Music" is still in the jazz repertory.—D.M.

INTRODUCTION

By Rudy Vallee

You may be surprised that I have undertaken to write an introduction to this book by my good friend Louis Armstrong, for in so many ways Louis and I are direct opposites.

Yet it is also true that the author and I have a great deal in common. I believe I was among the first to recognize his genius. It was before I ever saw him and heard some of his earlier records which have now become established milestones in the evolution of Swing Music, of which he was one of the great pioneers.

It was many years ago when I first saw Louis and felt his effect upon an audience. I was still a student at New Haven and was attending a performance of one of the famous colored shows of that day when I noticed in the pit with the orchestra a colored trumpet player who was reaching and "smacking out" high C's and even notes above that almost unreachable zenith. The audience was so fascinated that at times they forgot the show itself.

In the intervening years, Armstrong's amazing mastery of the trumpet has brought him world-wide fame and today he is generally regarded as one of the greatest, if not the very greatest, of all living trumpeters, particu-

larly, of course, in the high register. Volumes have been
written about Louis' virtuosity on this difficult instrument — the unerring purity of his notes, his lip and
fingering technique, and so on, which are, of course,
superb. But there is another side to the genius of Louis
Armstrong which I feel has not received the recognition
it deserves, and that is his most extraordinary style of
singing.

I said "singing" but it is almost inaccurate to use that
word to describe Louis' vocal renditions. Most of you
have heard his records, if you have not heard him, and
are familiar with that utterly mad, hoarse, inchoate
mumble-jumble that is Louis' "singing." And yet when
you study it, you will come to see that it is beautifully
timed and executed, and to perceive that a subtle musical understanding and keen mind are being manifest
through this seemingly incoherent expression. Armstrong's vocalizations are peculiarly Armstrong and as
distinct from the efforts of other artists as day is from
night. They often seem to be the result of a chaotic, dis-
organized mind struggling to express itself, but those
who know anything about modern music recognize his
perfect command of time spacing, of rhythm, harmony,
and pitch and his flawless understanding of the effects
he is striving to achieve. He is a master of his peculiar
art. To illustrate this, I suggest you listen to his recorded masterpiece, his vocalization of *I Surrender,
Dear*. You may say that it is not singing, that it is not
beauty, that a beautiful romantic song has been treated

as a madman would treat it, and I must, perforce, agree with you. If that is your reaction, try playing it a second, third or fourth time, and eventually there must dawn on you that this man knows what he is about and you will begin to feel upon you the sway of his extraordinary musical personality. It is a test of artistic work — repetition with a growth of effect.

That Armstrong's delightful, delicious sense of distortion of lyrics and melody has made its influence felt upon popular singers of our own day cannot be denied. Mr. Bing Crosby, the late Russ Columbo, Mildred Bailey, and many others, have adopted, probably unconsciously, the style of Louis Armstrong. Compare a record by Crosby, in which he departs from the "straight" form of the melody and lyric, and then listen to an Armstrong record and discover whence must have come some of his ideas of "swinging." Armstrong antedated them all, and I think that most of those artists who attempt something other than the straight melody and lyric as it is written, who in other words attempt to "swing," would admit, if they were honest with themselves and with their public, that they have been definitely influenced by the style of this master of swing improvisation.

That Louis will go on for many years delighting his audiences is, to my mind, a foregone conclusion. He is truly an artist, in every sense of the word, and that he has given so much happiness to his legion of devoted followers will one day merit his right to play for St. Peter a trumpet solo as only Armstrong can play one.

And then he may smile his wide smile and say, as he says so ludicrously in his recording of the tune of that name : "I hope Gabriel likes my music!"

There is no doubt in my mind as to what the answer will be.

CONTENTS

PART ONE

PART TWO

MUSIC SECTION
EDITED BY HORACE GERLACH

SWING THAT MUSIC

SWING THAT MUSIC

I. *JAZZ AND I GET BORN TOGETHER*

WHEN I fired off my daddy's old "38" it made the other kid's little six-shooter sound pretty sick. It banged out above the scatting of the firecrackers and the hot jazz music coming from the honky tonks down the street. It made a whole gang of sound, for sure.

It was New Year's Eve of 1913 and New Orleans was high, celebrating the way it always did—with bang and big time.

Merry-makers were going along the street and when that old cannon let loose in my hand, and sang out so loud, they stopped short and looked back. There was one pretty big party of them. They stood still a minute, then they all burst out laughing. They laughed a lot and then they called, "Happy New Year," and went on. I must have looked funny to them, a little kid with such a big gun in my hand, standing there scared half to death at all the noise I'd made.

But the really funny part of it was something very different. It was the way it all turned out. Because that shot, I do believe, started my career. It changed my life and brought me my big chance. In the twenty and more years that have passed since, I guess I have played almost all over the world. I played before the

Prince of Wales, the new King Edward, and his brother, the Duke of York, and the crown princess of Italy and for many other famous people, and I have swung my bands in Paris and Copenhagen and Brussels and Geneva and Vienna and New York and Chicago and Hollywood and many other places.   But whenever I have had a few minutes to myself out of all of this running around, so I could stop stock-still and ask myself, "Louis, how come this to happen to you?" I have always thought back to that one New Year's Eve before the big war, and of what followed.   For I was sent to jail.

Most people have some smell they like best and that depends a lot on what they got to like where they were born and brought up.   The nicest of all to me is the smell of a magnolia tree when it comes out in the late spring, in Louisiana.   Those big, white flowers do swing their scent.   They let it loose on the warm air and it spreads out over the whole county, and lies in the air for weeks, heavy and sweet.   That smell of magnolias is my earliest memory of home.

I was about five years old at that time.   I lived with my father and mother and my younger sister, Beatrice (we called her "Mamma Lucy") in the back-of-town part of New Orleans.   It was sort of a suburb called "James Alley."

My mother was a good and fine woman.   Her grandfather and grandmother had been slaves and she was born in a little town, about fifty miles from New Orleans, called Butte, Louisiana. She went to New Orleans when she was a little girl and when she grew up she became a house servant in a fine old white family. They called her Mary-Ann and she was part of the family and helped bring up all of their children till they were grown. She met my father in New Orleans. His name was Willie and he was a turpentine worker. My father died just a few years ago, but his mother is still living. She's a pretty old lady now — about ninety I guess — maybe more. I saw her when I was in New Orleans a little while ago. She certainly was one grand cook and could swing the biscuits. But I guess my father and mother were not very happy. He married her when she was only fifteen years old.

I was born on July 4, 1900, and my sister was born two years later. When I was five, my father and mother separated and my mother took me and "Mamma Lucy" to live right in the city with my great-grandmother. She was a very old lady and I remember her white hair. We moved to Liberty and Perdido Streets in what is called the Third Ward.

Were the kids bad in that neighborhood! My, my, my! They'd stay around the streets most of the night and were always shootin' dice and fighting. Pretty soon I got into their ways and my mother would try to talk to me and make me better. She told me never to steal and I never did. Every time I looked around I was in a fight with one of those kids. But I used to swing home mean "dukes" in those days, so, finally, they let me alone, mostly.   As I grew older I learned how to stay out of so many fights—then, too, I began to feel music in me. The new music called jazz was getting around.   They spelled it "jass" then.

Some of my friends liked to sing, so on warm nights we would go down to the Mississippi and sit on the docks and sing together.   Then we would perhaps take off our things and jump in and swim in and out around the big banana boats.   We were ready for swimming any time.   When we got tired of swimming we would sing some more, and that is the way I spent many evenings of my boyhood and I believe now it was a good way to spend them and kept me out of a lot of mischief.

When I was about thirteen years old I started up a singing quartet with three of the best singing boys from my neighborhood.   Believe me, we four were "singin' fools."   No kiddin'!   We went out big for the new jazz songs.

We used to go all through the pleasure sections of New Orleans, around the big hotels and night clubs and even the honky tonks or "gin mills," as they were called, and we would sing for the people, then pass the hat. We sang the new jazz songs, and got to learn how to sing them "hot."   The pennies and nickels and dimes just rolled into our little caps and then we would count them and divvy up and have some real nice change to take to our mothers.   My mother had taken care of my sister Lucy and me since we moved to the Third Ward — and that was eight years. Now I was able to take some care of them. Everything went well until that New Year's Eve of 1913. Our quartet was out hustling, as we called it, and the city was celebrating and we knew we stood good to take in a lot of change before the night was over.

As I said, New Orleans throws a heap of noise on New Year's Eve — they shoot off anything that's handy. My mother had an old "38" gun and when time came along towards New Year's she hid it away because she knew I'd get in trouble with it. Somehow I found it and on the big night, as our quartet was standing on the corner of Perdido and Rampart Streets singing, a boy passed us shooting off his little old six-shooter. So I told my boys, "Watch me show him up!"

I showed him up all right! A minute or so after I shot off that old gun, an old gray-haired detective came up behind me and hugged me and said, "You're under arrest!" The people who had laughed at me had turned down the street by then and didn't see it.

I know lots of men who are successful in life are always saying they owe their success to their hard knocks — and the harder the better. I think that's sometimes true and it sometimes isn't. But I do believe that my whole success goes back to that time I was arrested as a wayward boy at the age of thirteen. Because then I *had* to quit running around and began to learn something. Most of all, I began to learn music.

The Waif's Home for Boys was sort of like a boy's jail, but they didn't have routines like a jail. The boys wore overalls during the week and on Sundays we would dress up. And did we have to take orders! I'm telling you, it went mighty hard with me for a while, after being a kid that had had my way and come and gone as I wanted. But as the weeks rolled on I began to make myself feel at home.

In time, I came to think as much of that school as other men think of the college they went to, and I never go back to New Orleans now without paying the Home a nice visit and taking some little presents to the kids. I tell them to study and be good boys and they'll never be sorry they were sent there, but will be glad some day, as I am.

After a short while I had got so used to the Home that I forgot all about the streets. When the other kids started calling me nicknames I knew everything was all right. I have a pretty big mouth, so they hit on that, and began calling me Gatemouth or Satchelmouth, and that Satchelmouth has stuck to me all my life, except that now it's been made into "Satchmo" — "Satchmo" Armstrong.

Now, at the Home they had a little orchestra made up of the older boys — but I had no idea I'd ever be in it. I liked to sing but I didn't take music seriously so I could play an instrument. But that didn't come until later, and when it did it was the one biggest break in my life.

For a long time, from the first day I came, I caught the

THE BRASS BAND OF THE COLORED WAIF'S HOME FOR BOYS

NEW ORLEANS, 1913

"Little Louis" Armstrong, aged 13, is in the top row centre, holding his first trumpet

devil because of the neighborhood I came from and the bad children I had been going with.

There were all colored keepers at that time. A Mr. Jones was head keeper and there were two others, Mr. Alexander and Mr. Peter Davis. Mr. Alexander taught the boys gardening, practical painting and lots of things it was nice to learn. But somehow I liked Mr. Peter Davis best — for his music. His music ability was just the last word. He really knew his music, and it was he who trained the orchestra. He was very hard on me, for he thought I needed it, but it was Mr. Peter Davis who first saw possibilities in me. He would whip me every time he had a chance and every time he'd whip me he'd make these remarks, "You're one of those bad boys from Liberty and Perdido Streets and I don't like you." So I figured there wasn't any use saying anything to him. I just stood there and took my beatings like a little man. Pretty soon I became afraid of him — every time he'd pass by me, at the dinner table or wherever it was, I'd get a cold chill. It was that way for a long time.

Finally one day when we were all eating our supper at a long table, Mr. Peter Davis came down the line. I began to get nervous and, sure enough, when he got behind my seat he stopped. He touched me on the shoulder and said, "How'd you like to play in my band?"

Folks, I was so surprised I couldn't do a thing but gasp for breath, no foolin'.

Mr. Davis then called me off aside and told me that he had watched me real closely since I had been in the

Home and that he had come to the conclusion that I wasn't near as bad as the boys in my neighborhood. He said he realized that it wasn't my fault that my mother was poor and had to live where the rent was cheap, with two youngsters to care for. Mr. Davis also realized that I wasn't the type of boy who'd steal.

No Suh! My mother, Mary-Ann, always would say to me and my sister, Mamma Lucy, never to steal from anybody. It's not right and it's not necessary — and we never did. My mother always believed in the good old saying, "What's for you — you'll get it. Good things come to those who wait."

So Mr. Peter Davis decided to care a lot for me and put me in his Waif's Home Band. He taught me how to play the bugle first. I learned it very fast. Even then I could blow hard and I had just the right kind of deep chest and strong lips for brass horns of any old kind. In later years they called me "Iron Lips" Armstrong or "Brass Lips" because I could blow more high C notes in succession than any swing trumpeter in the world, they said. My record to date, as you may know, is two hundred and eighty high C notes. I go into the high C when I am swinging a good hot number and feel my orchestra going to town behind me. I like to get way up there and hold on to that clear high note.

But to get back. Mr. Davis first taught me the bugle calls, the Mess Call, Taps, in fact, the whole routine of calls. Then he made me the bugler of the band. I had to blow a call for about everything the boys did. You never saw anything like it — they could hardly make a move without my blowing 'em to it. But it gave me good practice and I did so well with the bugle that Mr. Davis promoted me to learn the trumpet! And right there my future stretched out shining clear ahead of me, though, of course, I didn't see it then.

Jazz is the granddaddy of today's swing music and though they both came from the same soil, along the lower Mississippi, they have come to be very different kinds of music, as any good musician knows and any good dancer feels. But I will talk about these differences later. What I want to say now is that jazz had been taking hold of people. It had come up slowly out of the old negro folk songs and the spirituals, and the regular beat of the jazz syncopation probably came out of the strumming of the banjoes which the slaves had learned to play before the Civil War. Some say it went back to the tom-toms of our people in Africa before we were civilized. And it might be.

Anyway, the Mississippi delta country around New Orleans was the birthplace of jazz and it was New Orleans which first went crazy about it.

Only four years before I learned to play the trumpet in the Waif's Home, or in 1909, the first great jazz orchestra was formed in New Orleans by a cornet player named Dominick James LaRocca. They called him

"Nick" LaRocca. His orchestra had only five pieces, but they were the hottest five pieces that had ever been known before. LaRocca named this band, "The Old Dixieland Jazz Band." He had an instrumentation different from anything before — an instrumentation that made the old songs sound new. Besides himself at the cornet, LaRocca had Larry Shields, clarinet, Eddie Edwards, trombone, Regas, piano, and Sbarbaro, drums. They all came to be famous players and the Dixieland Band has gone down now in musical history. Some of the great records they made, which carried the new jazz music all over the world in those days were: *Tiger Rag, Lazy River, Clarinet Marmalade, Ostrich Walk, Sensation, Livery Stable Blues* and *Toddlin' Blues*. LaRocca retired a few years ago to his home in New Orleans but his fame as one of the great pioneers of syncopated music will last a long, long time, as long, I think, as American music lives.

But at the time I am now writing of, 1913, when I was still a boy in the Waif's Home just learning to toot, the Dixieland Band was getting to be known about far beyond New Orleans, and it was only three years later, in 1916, that LaRocca opened up at Reisenweber's restaurant in New York. That was before the United States went into the War, of course, and people in the East were dancing to the kind of sweet and soft ballroom music that Meyer Davis and other famous northern ballroom conductors of that time had perfected. That was also not so long after Mr. and Mrs. Vernon Castle had set the whole country crazy with their famous "Castle Walk." They were the greatest ballroom dance team ever known up to the time of Mr. Fred Astaire and his sister, Adele, and later, of course, Mr. Astaire and Miss Ginger Rogers.

The Dixieland Band changed everything. Pretty soon LaRocca was taking in as much as a thousand dollars a night and all of New York was strummin' *Lazy Daddy*, *Sensation* and *Toddlin' Blues*. The boys would put a tin can painted "Sugar" out on the dance floor in front of them and when the people got to dancing hot with the music they'd throw money into the sugar can, plenty. That's how the Dixieland's new music stirred people up in those days. Jazz had "gone East" and made good, and LaRocca really took it there and first put it across. It made an easier road for all the others who were very soon to come. A year or so later the Dixieland went to London and had the same success. London kept them there more than a year.

After their triumph in the East and abroad, the Dixieland Band never went back to New Orleans. In fact, the great combination broke up before 1922. All the boys had made more money than they ever dreamed there was. Maybe they didn't want any more — anyhow they broke up. Larry Shields came home before I left New Orleans. He put his money into a business. Later, as I said, LaRocca came home, too.

Very few of the men whose names have become great in the early pioneering of jazz and of swing were trained in music at all. They were *born* musicians, they felt their music and played by ear and memory. That was the way it was with the great Dixieland Five. None of them could read. But they *were* musicians and they made the world say so.

That reminds me I must not fail to mention right here a boy named Buddy Bolden. So far as any of us know who were born and brought up in New Orleans, and just about saw jazz born, this boy was really the first of them all. He blazed himself into New Orleans with his cornet, as early as 1905, and they tell me people thought he was plumb crazy the way he tossed that horn. Buddy got to drinking too much—staying up two or three nights a week without sleep and going right on to work again, just like many hot musicians. They get low in their minds and drink some more. Too many of them go to pieces when they're young, like Buddy. Bolden used to blow so loud and strong that, on a still day, they say, you could hear him a mile away. The sad part of that is that Bolden actually did go crazy a few years later and is still in an insane asylum at Jackson, Mississippi. But before he got sick, he was a rage at all the smart private parties in town. He was gone, as I remember, when the Dixieland came along. But while Bolden was undoubtedly the first great individual jazz player, he never had a band like the Dixieland and he never got to be known outside of New Orleans. He was just a one-man genius that was ahead of 'em all—too good for his time.

Around 1909, when the Dixieland started cutting the hot new music, a whole lot of players began to take it up in the cabarets and pretty soon New Orleans was clean mad with it. Many of the old plantation songs and the popular tunes of the day were being played in the new jazz rhythms and new tunes were being composed that were hotter and better. All of a sudden came along those two great songs, *Memphis Blues* and *St. Louis Blues*. My, they were hot and how we all loved them! They were written by a colored composer named W. C. Handy who lived in Memphis. He had caught jazz from some of the players on the Mississippi River boats. Handy's name will go down as long as jazz does because of those two early songs, if for nothing else. He lives today in Harlem, New York, and has his own music publishing house and every jazz musician everywhere honors him.

After that, nothing much was played but the new-style music. From the big smart cabarets down to the lowest honky tonks and gin mills, it was all jazz, and the players who could do best at it were in great demand.

One of the front men was Joe Oliver who was later to be known as "King" Oliver and of all the others of that day "Papa Joe," as I have always called him, was the one who was to travel farthest along the road that the old Dixieland pioneered. I am going to tell you more about the "King" later on. He was a big man with a whole gang o' horn.

Another great New Orleans orchestra of that time

was right on the heels of the Dixieland and that was Freddy Keppard's "Creole Band." Freddy was ace trumpeter and had a guitarist, a trombonist, a bass violinist and "Big Eye" Louis at the clarinet. They trailed LaRocca's five to New York and opened at the famous Winter Garden there.

But the Creole Band broke up, too, after some years, and I believe "Big Eye" Louis is the only one still living, though I'm not dead sure. Those boys burned themselves up soon in those days.

You'll notice that none of the early orchestras used either the piano or saxophone. In fact, the sax just came into general use as late as about 1917. Often as not they didn't even use drums.

One of the hottest clarinetists then was a young genius named Sydney Bachet. He is now a featured man with Noble Sissle's Band, playing soprano sax. Bachet teamed up with Ed Atkins, trombone, and the pair of them struck out from New Orleans to see the world. They actually got to London ahead of the Dixieland, which arrived about the end of 1917, and those two boys took old London by storm. Nobody there had ever heard anything like it. Later on Bachet toured the Continent with Jim Europe's band.

Two others of that day were Buddy Peete and Joe ("Wingy") Mannone. Buddy played cornet. He didn't last long and not many people now ever heard of him. He burned himself out, I guess, and died, but he was good while he lived. "Wingy" Monnone went on to success. He has made many swing records and today his five-piece swing combination is a star attraction at the "Hickory House," which is one of New York's real swing centers, and swing musicians go there to hear them play, especially on Sunday afternoons.

Among others of that original group of great players who lived jazz, slept jazz, ate jazz and brought jazz into being, I must mention Emmanuel Perez who played hot trumpet. Emmanual couldn't speak so much English but, boy, his horn could talk in *any* man's language! He didn't have an orchestra — he had a ten-piece brass band. It was composed as follows : three trumpets, two trombones, alto horn, baritone horn, E-flat clarinet, bass drum and snare drum. He called it the "Onward Brass Band." He began playing jazz, in brass, about 1910 — I remember as a kid of ten years old I was so crazy about Perez' brass band I would follow them on the streets when they paraded with the Elks and Moose and other societies. Now the marching brass bands in the North never went in for jazz — always straight march time and all that. But in New Orleans it was different. All the brass bands would swing jazz like the orchestras — even the drummer had a swing.

There were a whole lot of brass bands in New Orleans then. On big days, lodge parades and things like that, all the brass bands would turn out and try to outdo each other. That's when you heard *some* music. Down there everybody was music crazy. I used to follow brass bands all day.

And later on, after I left the Waif's Home, I joined one of them, the Tuxedo Brass Band. Often we'd play at funerals. We'd play sad music when we took them to the grave; then, when the brother was buried and we were bringing them back to the Lodge Hall, we'd play swing music, because they needed cheering up.

"King" Oliver played his trumpet in Perez Brass Band and also had his own orchestra, "The Magnolia," and this was another of the finest in New Orleans. His instrumentation, I remember very well, was ace trumpet (Oliver himself), clarinet, trombone, guitar, bass violin, violin and drums — seven pieces.

When New Orleans began to go red hot like this, jazz began to spread, little by little, onto the big excursion boats that used to play the Mississippi River ports, as far up, and farther, than St. Paul. They were something like the old Show Boats of Civil War days.

Up the Mississippi, from New Orleans to St. Paul, from the river on to Chicago, from Chicago west to San Francisco and from Chicago east to New York. That was the path jazz followed. But it took a whole quarter of a century for it to make the trip — and to bring it finally to the music we know today as *swing music*. And the changes it has gone through in those years — and I've been with them all — are plenty, believe me.

II. *IN THE TRAIL OF*
"THE DIXIELAND FIVE"

WHEN Mr. Peter Davis decided to make me into a trumpeter for the Waif's Home Band, he took me to his little office where he kept the band instruments and said, "Louis, I am going to give you something which I want you to be very careful with — you be good to it and it'll be good to you." Then he got out a trumpet and put it in my hand.

I have had a score or more of beautiful and expensive trumpets, gold ones and silver ones, presented to me since, including the gold one with ivory valves given to me at the Palladium Theatre in London and which I use mostly over the radio now, but I've never had one that gave me the kick that first cheap horn gave me. I was so happy I guess I must have grinned clear out to my ears. And did I take to that trumpet! Boy! I couldn't let it lay. In less than no time I was jazzing up *Home, Sweet Home*.

Mr. Davis saw that that trumpet and me were going to be pals and he helped me with my fingering and breathing and mouth work. Then very soon, maybe to encourage me more, he made me leader of the whole band. I had a different uniform from the other boys. If they'd have blue coats with white trousers, I would have cream-colored coat and blue trousers, all different.

I improved so much with this band that Mr. Davis began to be proud of us. He began to take us to out-ings and to street parades in New Orleans. We were glad to get a chance to see the streets of the city again and we'd never get tired of playing so we could go.

In the summer we would play for picnics and then we would go out to the fair grounds where there would be big crowds of people from all over the State. It was my first experience playing to a crowd and it taught me I couldn't dare be afraid but had to stick right to my playing and not think of the rest.

I remember one spring day when our little band went to play for a small picnic some ways out in the country and across the river. Mr. Davis had some business in New Orleans and couldn't go along as he always did, so he put me in charge. Before we left he told me he trusted me to see that everything went right and that we would play good. He said, "Louie, I know I can count on you." I said, "Yes, Mr. Davis, you sure can." And I loved him so much because of all he had done for me that I knew he could.

We boys had to meet the picnic party up the river near to Baton Rouge and when we arrived and knew we were in sight we took our band formation and marched in smart. They gave us a nice cheer and treated us fine and then we all ferried across the river. The Mississippi there is very wide and flat and muddy and there is a powerful sweep of water down the middle. But it's an *Ol' Man River* when it gets down around

New Orleans. A little farther down it hits the delta
and then it spreads out and loses its strength, like a
dying old man, before it runs off into the sea. That big
river has always made me a little sad and I think that
is so with all the people who have lived down near the
delta. Mr. Jerome Kern sure knew what he was doing
when he wrote *Ol' Man River,* for Miss Ferber's "Show
Boat." He must have been down there.

Our picnic party landed on the low, yellow-mud bank
on the other side and very soon we were in pretty country. As I have said, it was spring and the azaleas were
blooming, white and pink and red. I spoke before about
the magnolias, and the next sweetest, to me at least, are
the azaleas. Some people like them best. I guess there
are hundreds of different kinds of flowers in New Orleans
in the spring. Folks who live in the North don't know
what it's like. Everywhere you go are flowers. The
walls and fences and sides of the houses and the balconies
out over the streets are covered over with vines blooming
with flowers of many kinds. The magnolias come a little
later on after most of the others are gone, like a featured
actress who's got to have the stage to herself and can dish
it out alone.

The azaleas often grow right up near to a cypress
swamp and sometimes, if the swamp isn't too very wet
for them, they grow all on through it. There was a
cypress swamp near by the place our picnic stopped to
spread the lunch and rest, and I could see the azalea
plants were blooming inside.

The folks who were giving the picnic were very kind to us kids. We played for them — everything they asked for — and then they invited us to sit down and partake of all of the good things they had brought along. I'll never forget that feast because we only had very plain food at the Home and this was a real treat for us. Oh man! They gave us fine cured ham, and sweet, fried chicken wings, and spoon bread and potato-pie, and cold biscuits spread with pecan butter and other good things. We just stuffed our little stomachs and felt fine.

After the lunch the picnic folks wanted to laze around and be quiet, and so I told the boys they didn't have anything to do for awhile and could break up if they wanted to. I had my own mind set on that cypress swamp.

As I walked across the field, the sun felt mighty hot on my head — and I can take a lot of sun. But as soon as I reached the swamp and got inside it was cooler. Going into a real cypress swamp is something like going into a church, I always think. It's cool and quiet, and sort of gloomy, and you can't hear yourself walk. There's a high roof way over your head where the tops of the trees come together, all covered over thick with Spanish moss so that very little daylight gets through. The swamp is all cut up with little winding streams of black water running every old way, and they make paths through the trees like the aisles of a church, only not straight. The moss hangs down from the trees everywhere and almost reaches the ground and it's partly the moss and partly the knees, I guess, that makes a cypress swamp so scarey. These knees are the roots of the cypress trees which come up out of the ground like a man's knee and go back down again. Any good sized cypress tree will swing up twenty or thirty or more knees, so that the swamp is just covered with them. That's one reason why it's bad to be caught in a cypress swamp after dark. Everywhere you turn, you're stumbling across those knees and maybe falling into one of those streams of black water. The slaves who ran away used to hide in the swamps and it was hard to catch them. But nobody could live there very long, I am sure — at nights they would go crazy. But I liked to go into the swamps in the daytime, in the spring and summer.

I fooled around a little, chucked a stone at a big black snake I saw slipping down the side of a bank, and missed him, and then I got sleepy, with all I had eaten, and decided I would take myself a little nap. I settled down comfortable between two cypress knees, where the moss was thick and soft, and pretty soon I was asleep.

The hot day and the excitement of being in charge of the band all alone, and all, must have made me pretty tired because I slept all through the afternoon. When I woke up I was sure scared. It was dark. I could just see the trees right next to me. I got up to my feet and there I was, all turned around and not knowing which way I could go. Then I began to remember stories I had heard about people being lost in the swamp and

wandering around for days until they fell into a bog
and never came out. I rubbed my hand across my
forehead and it was all sweaty. I felt weak and sat down
again on the ground, to try to think what I could do.
Finally I heard a shout. It sounded far off. I knew
it must be my boys looking for me. I got up and after
a while followed the shouts, stumbling here and there
over the knees and pulling up short when I'd run my face
into some hanging moss. Pretty soon I got to the edge
and was I surprised! It was just late sunset outside!
The folks were all packed up and ready to go, so I said
I was sorry to hold them back and we went on down to
the ferry. But I didn't play music any more that day.

One morning, after I had been at the Waif's Home
about a year and a half, Mr. Peter Davis called me to his
office. He said, "Louie, get your trumpet and call the
roll because we're saying goodbye to somebody who's
going home." So I called the boys together and we
wondered who was going to leave us. When we were
all together in the hall, the Head Keeper got up and
cleared his throat and said that there was one of us
who had learned how to be a good boy again and that
because he had worked so hard and had good behavior
they had decided he could go home. All of us kids
were looking around at each other, trying to think who
it could be. Then the Head Keeper said, "I know
you'll all be glad to know it's 'Little Louie' Armstrong
who is going home, and I am sure you will all wish him

good luck. His mother is here now to get him. Louie," he said, looking over at me, "go get your things together."

Well, you can imagine my surprise. I was mighty glad to see my dear mother. Bless her heart! she went through an awful lot for "Mamma Lucy" and me. And she wasn't so old herself—just twenty-nine years old at that time.

I found out later that what the Head Keeper said about the Home having decided to let me go wasn't just true and probably I'd have been at the Home a lot longer if it hadn't been for Mary-Ann, my mother. Ever since I had been sent away, which nearly broke her heart at that time, because, she said, there had not ever been any scandal in her family, she had been talking to the white people she worked for about how I was really a good boy. She had worked for them for ten years then and they thought a lot of her and their children did. They were very fine people, so finally they started working to get me out and talked to Judge Wilson who had sent me to the Home in the first place. So when my mother came out to the Home that day to get me she had a written release signed by Judge Wilson. My, she was happy! But of course the Head Keeper wanted the other kids to think that it was his doing—and that was all right. Many years later, when I went back to New Orleans and had made good, old Judge Wilson was very kind to me. He made a speech out at the Home and told the boys they should use me "as an example"

and some day they might do something, too. I told
Judge Wilson that he did the best thing for me he
could have done and he said he thought that was a fine
way for me to feel and he had watched my career and
would always be glad to see me back in New Orleans.
It made me proud.

So I put on my little cheap suit and went home with
my mother. When we got home, she had a big pot of
red beans and rice all cooked for me. And believe me,
I nearly killed myself. My mother could cook real good.

After supper she sat down and gave me a long talk.
She said to me, "Son, you must promise me you'll be a
good boy from this day on, and try to make a man of
yourself." And I said I would.

The very next day, I went out looking for a job. I
was fourteen years of age when I got out of the Waif's
Home. I could play trumpet pretty good by now, but
because of my being so young I figured bands or orchestras wouldn't want me. I couldn't find any real job,
so I started selling newspapers. I got that through a
little white kid named Paul. His big brother had a
newsstand and since Paul and I were kids together, and
we'd got along so good together, Paul didn't have much
trouble putting in a good word for me.

I used to make some nice money for a kid of fourteen.
Every now and then me and some of the other newsboys
would have a little friendly game of dice. Most of the
time, I'd "take 'em"—meaning I would win all the

money. Then sometimes, of course, they'd wash me just as clean. When I'd win I'd take the money home to my mother.

While I was a newsboy I got a chance at a steady job at the Cloverland dairy, and I took it and went to work there for a while.

I can remember just as well, I was seventeen years of age before I decided to pick up my cornet again. Everybody was playing cornet then, but "King" Oliver, "Papa Joe" to me, was way out in front of all of them as the very best. He was ace cornet player with Kid Ory's Jazz Orchestra, which was now the top orchestra in New Orleans and the best seven-piece jazz band there had been since the Dixieland Band had left. They played in a big cabaret down in the pleasure district. Kids were not allowed in those places. But I had to hear "King" Oliver play, so I would put on a pair of my step-daddy's pants (I forgot to say my mother had married again) at night and would stand outside of the cabaret by the bandstand so I could hear him on that cornet. He used to blow his horn out of the window, so I could get a good load of how he dished it out to the folks inside. Gee! that was really a "sender" to me.

"King" Oliver was so powerful he used to blow a cornet out of tune every two or three months. My! how that man used to blow. I was constantly hanging around after "King" Oliver. I looked towards him as though he were some kind of a god, or something similar. Between the years of 1914, when I got out of the Home, and 1917, I never missed hearing him play his music. He was my inspiration.

The biggest kick of my life was when "Papa Joe" invited me to come up to his house and go to the store for his missus. He took such a liking to me he started giving me lessons and answered anything I wanted to know. He taught me the modern way of phrasing on the cornet and trumpet.

When people began to see the big "King" Oliver was looking out for me and helping me they began to think maybe I could play pretty good. After a few months, when somebody would need a cornet player they would say, "Go get 'Little Louie.'" That was my pet name at the time, because I was so small and young.

Then the big time came when myself and Little Joe Lindsay organized our own little jazz band. It was the first time I'd had a band of my own. Lindsay played hot drums and I played cornet. The rest of the instrumentation consisted of clarinet, trombone, guitar and bass violin — six pieces, and how we used to swing! We had the hottest band for a bunch of youngsters just starting out that there was. Yes, suh! We kids copied our instrumentation after the Kid Ory Band which featured "King" Oliver, and we copied their style, too, as far as we could.

About that time, Miss Ethel Waters brought a show to New Orleans, sort of a revue. A pianist named Fletcher Henderson was the conductor of the orchestra in the theatre she played at. I mention him in passing because later he went to New York and became very successful. He was friendly to me when I was starting out, and he did a lot for me later because it was through Fletcher I got my first opening on Broadway in New York, more than ten years later.

Us boys went up into the peanut gallery to see Miss Waters. She was very young and was wonderful even then, but of course not so wonderful or famous as she is now. A whole lot of very noted musicians and entertainers have started in that country, as you can see.

About a year later, a break came for me and I took another big step forward. Luck sure swings a lot of punch in life . . . but you've got to be ready to grab hold of it when it comes around.

Well, what happened was that "Papa Joe" decided to move on to Chicago and have a big band up there where jazz was now beginning to go very big. That left Kid Ory without his ace cornet. They looked around town for somebody, and then Kid Ory decided that even though I was only eighteen years old I was probably the only one who could take Joe Oliver's place. And so I became a member of my first real fine and top-notch orchestra. Was I full of chest! My, my, my! I was so happy and proud, you can't know. Now I was a *real* musician, no more playin' around with a kid band but just being right in there with the men I'd looked up to, and even almost worshipped.

"Papa Joe" went on up to Chicago and had a big or-

chestra there and was making a smash hit.   Chicago was
just like New York and London and other places; none
of them had ever heard the kind of music that came up
out of New Orleans in those days.   Chicago got it first.

The men I knew as a boy started it all.   Whatever it's
good for, and however long it will live, swing music
was born in my country; it seeded there in New
Orleans and grew there, and there it got so hot it
had to burst out and it did, and spread to the world.

III. *WHAT IS "SWING"?*

THERE are millions of people who don't like or do not yet understand American jazz music; in fact, I know, they seem to hate it. They do not seem to see the difference between trashy, popular jazz and fine swing music. Maybe they're so sick of cheap, bad jazz, they don't care any more. So they will turn off their radios when a fine swing orchestra starts to play. They would rather hear some "sweet" band play, the kind all "hot" musicians call "corney." I don't know why it is. It has often made me very sorry. I think they do not understand.

I do know that a musician who plays in "sweet" orchestras must be like a writer who writes stories for some popular magazines. He has to follow along the same kind of line all the time, and write what he thinks the readers want just because they're used to it. That keeps him writing the same kind of thing year after year. But a real swing musician never does that. He just plays, feels as he goes, and swings as he feels. I think that must have been the way the greatest writers did, too. I'm sure they didn't think only about what people wanted to have them write — they went on swinging their stuff; let it fall, let it lay, it's what it is. They liked best to write just the way they felt. And I think that's probably why they *were* great.

In the same way, that it why I think real swing musicians are great, even though you might not ever hear about many of them.   They start in and play for their fun.   Each one plays the instrument he likes best and plays it in his own way, with everything in him.   If one of them is real lucky and has the breaks and finally gets to be well known and makes some money, well, it's so much velvet then, Oh, man!

But most of the boys never do.   Buddy Bolden was only one of many truly great swing players I have known who never got to be heard of outside a small circle. Only musicians know about them.   It's because of that that I mention so much the many lucky breaks I have had in my life.   Without them, I might right now be blowing a horn back in a Third Ward honky tonk. That I know very well.   Don't think I don't.

For a man to be a good swing conductor he should have been a swing player himself, for then he knows a player is no good if the leader sets down on him too much and doesn't let him "go to town" when he feels like going.   That phrase, "goin' to town," means cuttin' loose and takin' the music with you, whatever the score may call for.   Any average player, if he's worth anything at all, can follow through a score, as it's written there in front of him on his instrument rack.   But it takes a swing player, and a real good one, to be able to leave that score and to know, or "feel," just when to leave it and when to get back on it.   No conductor can tell him, because it all happens in a second and doesn't happen the same way any two times running. It is just that liberty that every individual player must have in a real swing orchestra that makes it most worth listening to. Every time they play there is something new swinging into the music to make it "hot" and interesting. And right here I want to explain that "hot," as swing musicians use the word, does not necessarily mean loud or even fast. It is used when a swing player gets warmed up and "feels" the music taking hold of him so strong that he can break through the set rhythms and the melody and toss them around as he wants without losing his way. That creates new effects and is done whether the music is loud or soft or fast or slow.

You will think that if every man in a big sixteen-piece band had is own way and could play as he wanted, that all you would get would be a lot of jumbled up, crazy noise. This would be and is true with ordinary players, and that is why most bands have to play "regular" and their conductors can't dare let them leave their music as it is scored. The conductor himself may decide on certain variations, an "arrangement" they call it, but the players have to follow that scoring. In that way the conductor or "arranger" may write some "hot" phrasing into an old score and, to those who don't know, the orchestra may seem to be "swinging." But when you've got a real bunch of swing players together in an orchestra, you can turn them loose for the most part. "Give 'em their head," as they say of a race horse. They all play together, picking up and following each other's "swing-ing," all by ear and sheer musical instinct. It takes a very fine ear and some years of playing to do that. That is why there have been so few really fine swing orches-tras in the world. First you have to get a combination of natural swing players and then they've got to learn how to play in and out together as one man. No con-ductor can *make* them do it, or even show them much how to. His biggest part is to make suggestions and try to get them into a good humor and then let them alone. And I mean alone ! If he doesn't ; if he starts telling one man just how to play this part and another how to play another part, pretty soon he'll ruin his orchestra and he'll have one that just plods along with the score, playing regular, and all the life will be gone out of the men. Swing players have got to have a good time when they are playing and they can't have a good time, playing and rehearsing as they do twelve and fourteen hours a day, if you just make machines out of them.

No man in my band which you hear over the radio *has* to do anything, except be a good musician and "show" on time and in good shape for rehearsals. If he *can't* play away from the score, I don't want him. He doesn't belong in a real swing band, and, Heaven knows, there are plenty of fine non-swing or "regular" bands in the land which will be glad enough to have him. My men know that — and my knowing it may be the biggest reason why we are out in front today. If I hadn't come up myself as a swing trumpeter, and found out that you've got to be let alone and allowed to play your own way, probably I would be bearing down more on my boys and flattening out their style; and they would not be happy because they all know better.

So if you have been hearing about swing music, but have not known much about the difference, listen closely when you hear one of the big "regular" orchestras playing on the air or in your favorite hotel or club, and then listen carefully to a swing orchestra like Benny Goodman's or Jimmy Dorsey's or the Casa Loma or the Louis Armstrong Band. Pretty soon you will begin to notice that all of the players in the "regular" orchestra are playing almost perfectly together to a regular, set, rhythmic beat, and are smoothly following the melody to the end. No one instrument will be heard standing out at any time during the piece (unless, of course, there happens to be a soloist leading them for a number). Then when you listen to a swing band, you will begin to recognize that all through the playing of the piece, individual instruments will be heard to stand out and then retreat and you will catch new notes and broken-up rhythms you are not at all familiar with. You may have known the melody very well but you will never have heard it played just that way before and will never hear it played just that way again. Because the boys are "swinging" around, and away from, the regular beat and melody you are used to, following the scoring very loosely and improvising as they go, by ear and free musical feeling. If you pay attention for a little while, you will easily notice the difference.   You will probably feel differently, too — the "regular" style music will relax you but the swing is likely to make you feel keen — waiting on edge for the "hot" variations you feel are coming up at any moment.   That is because you recognize, maybe without knowing it, that something really creative is happening right before you.

Well, I started in playing hot cornet in Kid Ory's Band, taking "King" Oliver's place.   You will remember I was eighteen years old then.

We had plenty to do all of the time.   Rich people were always giving dinners and parties at their homes or in the big hotels and we were in great demand because the band was considered the best in town.   Once or twice a week we would play out at the New Orleans Country Club, out in the West End.   Often we would be asked to play at Tulane University for the college dances, or proms.   The young people were keen on our music and more than anything I would enjoy playing for them, as I still do.   About that time I worked up a little "Jive" routine, which was a little tap dancing and a little fooling around between numbers to get laughs. That routine came in handy later on in my first year in Chicago.

Fletcher Henderson who I told you had played for Miss Ethel Waters that time had gone to New York by now, and one day I got a letter asking me to join him there.   I was always afraid to leave New Orleans;

afraid, I guess, that I'd lose my job and couldn't get back home. I wasn't like Syd Bachet and others who struck out when they were young. I wanted to stay near home. So when Fletcher asked me that first time, I talked it over with Zutti, the drummer, who was a pal of mine. Zutti didn't know what to say so I decided if he could go with me I might go. I wrote Fletcher I could come if my friend could have a job too. But Fletcher did not have an opening for a drummer, so I did not go to New York — not until a good many years later, when Fletcher Henderson asked me again. I think it turned out for the best that I did not go East at that time. I still had a lot to learn about jazz playing and there in New Orleans, and later on the river boats and on Chicago's South Side, I was living and working all the time around men who could teach me what I needed. Often it's better, I am sure, to come on a little slowly. You'll probably last a lot longer.

In the meantime, "King" Oliver would write to me quite often from Chicago. He told me that some day he would send for me to come with him there. But it was some time before he had a chance and not until I had had another experience, that taught me more and more about my music. I became trumpeter in a twelve-piece orchestra on a big Mississippi excursion boat.

My river life on that boat (it lasted for two years) is one of my happiest memories and was very valuable to me. It all grew out of a funny accident — another of the breaks I said I have had. Kid Ory's Band had been engaged one evening to play on a truck that was to drive through the streets advertising some big dance. They were always advertising like that with trucks and bands in New Orleans. Well, we were playing a red-hot tune when another truck came along the street with another hot band. We came together at that same corner of Rampart and Perdido Streets where I had been arrested five years before and sent to the Waif's Home. Of course that meant war between the two bands and we went to it, playing our strongest. I remember I almost blew my brains through my trumpet.

A man was standing on the corner listening to the "fight." When we had finally outplayed the other band, this man walked over and said he wanted to speak with me. It was "Fate" Marable, a noted hot pianist and leader of the big band on the excursion steamer *Dixie Belle*. He said he had heard me blow and wanted me for his band. So we made a deal and I signed up with Marable. It was in November of 1919. I had been with Kid Ory at the Peter Lalas Cabaret at Iberville and Maris Streets for sixteen months. I had learned a lot from Ory and had begun to get a little reputation, in a small sort of way, as a hot trumpeter. But while I could play music, like most of the others I couldn't read it much yet — just a little. I had made my mind up I wanted to learn.

It may sound funny that I was so quick to leave Kid Ory and sign up for the boat with "Fate" Marable, as though I were just running out on Ory after the big chance he had put my way and all he had done for me. The excursion boats had a big name in those days. They played the Mississippi ports away up to St. Paul and beyond. When they went North on these trips they always had white orchestras, but, for the first time, it was planned that year to take a colored orchestra along on the *Dixie Belle* when she shoved off in the spring on her trip North. I guess that was because the colored orchestras that had been coming up strong in New Orleans in the last few years, like Kid Ory's, were so hot and good that they were getting a real reputation. The chance to be with that first colored jazz band to go North on the river might have turned any kid's head at nineteen. But even that wouldn't have been enough to make me leave Ory. I wanted to get away from New Orleans for another reason and that was because I was not happy there just then.

Ten months before, when I was eighteen, I got married. I had married a handsome brown-skinned girl from Algiers, La., named Daisy Parker. We two kids should never have been married. We were too young to understand what it meant. I had to be up most of the night every night, playing in the orchestra, and in that way I neglected her, but I was so crazy about music that I couldn't think about much else. I see now it must have gone hard with a young and pretty girl up from a small town. And was she pretty! She naturally wanted to come ahead of everything else and she had a very high temper, partly, I guess, because she was so young and inexperienced. And in that same way I was quick to resent her remarks, so, as I say, we were not happy—in fact we were very unhappy, both of us. I think young folks feel those things a lot worse than people a little older—after they fuss and quarrel they are more hurt and it lasts longer. Today my first wife and I are very good friends and have a great deal of respect for each other. We look back on those days and just say it was too bad we were so young and headstrong when we were married. But we both know, too, we did love each other and tried hard—and that is the funny part of it, and the sad part.

Ory knew all about our troubles. He had done his best to help smooth us out, but maybe nobody could have. So when he found I had the chance to go with that fine band on the river for awhile, he understood it would be a good thing.

New Orleans, of course, was the hottest and gayest city on the Mississippi then, even including St. Louis, so all through the winter months, from November until April, when the weather is not so hot and New Orleans is at its highest, the excursion boats would stay right there, running dance excursions up and down the river every night and tying up in the daytime.

The steamer *Dixie Belle* was one of the biggest and best of them. She had her berth at the foot of Canal Street. The orchestra would start playing at eight o'clock while she was at the wharf, to attract people, and then she would shove out into the river at eight-thirty every night with a big crowd on board and cruise slowly around until about eleven o'clock when she would come back in. The *Dixie Belle* was fixed up inside something like a dance hall. She was a paddle-wheeler, with great paddle wheels on each side, near the middle, and she had big open decks and could hold a lot of people.

So all that winter, which was the winter of 1919 and 1920, we cruised there around New Orleans and every night when we pulled in, of course I would go home to Daisy. Sometimes we were very happy and I would hate to think of April coming, when I was to go north on the boat.

The orchestra on the *Dixie Belle* was, as I have said, a twelve-piece orchestra and every man was a crackshot musician. "Fate" Marable had recruited them from the best bands in town, taking this man here and that one there and each one because he was a "hot" player on his own particular instrument. "Fate" was a fine swing pianist, himself, and he knew that in time they would learn to play together. Now the most famous jazz orchestras of that day, as you will remember, had had no more than six or seven pieces (though some of the pure brass bands, the marching bands, had more). The old "Dixieland" had only five pieces and so had Freddy Keppard's "Creole Band." "King" Oliver's famous "Magnolia" and Kid Ory's Band had seven pieces each. So, you see, twelve pieces *was* big.

Winter passed and finally April came. The *Dixie*

Belle was all cleaned out and fixed up with new paint and polish and finally the day came for us to start up the river. My mother and "Mamma Lucy" came down to see us off, but Daisy wasn't there. We had had another quarrel.

As we pulled out into the river and turned north, I began to feel funny, wishing one minute they'd left me back on the wharf and feeling keen the next moment that I was going. The sweeping of the paddle wheels got louder and louder as we got going. It seemed they had never made so much noise before — they were carrying me away from New Orleans for the first time.

In the seven months to come, I was to follow the Mississippi for nearly two thousand miles and visit many places. It was a handful of travelling, believe me, for a kid who'd always been afraid to leave home before.

IV. *UP THE MISSISSIPPI*

WE shoved away early in the morning so we could make Baton Rouge, our first stop, by night-down. It was a run of about eighty miles, upstream. A few passengers were on board, as it was to be a day trip, although the *Dixie Belle* was not meant to be a boat for regular passenger travel but only for big excursion parties, so she was not fitted out with many staterooms.

It was a warm spring day and the river was high with water, but not flooding. The musicians did not have much to do except laze around on the decks and watch the shores, or now and then throw a little dice or something. After a while, when we had had our last look at New Orleans, I found myself a nice corner up on the top deck right under the pilot house and settled down with my trumpet and a polishing rag. I had bought myself a fine new instrument just before starting out, but even that wasn't shiny enough for *this* trip. No, suh ! So I took the rag and shined her a little and then I put her to my mouth and tried out a few blasts. She sounded strong and sweet, with a good pure tone. I swung a little tune and saw we were going to get along fine together. So then I rubbed her up some more, taking my time, until I was satisfied. Over on the left shore a great cypress swamp was passing slowly by —

there must have been hundreds of miles of it, stretching away off to the west — dark and hung all over with Spanish moss.   I felt very happy where I was.   The sun was just warm enough, the chunking of the paddle wheels was now pleasant to hear and everything was peaceful. Pretty soon I spread the rag on the deck beside me and lay my new trumpet on it and began to think of how lucky I really was.   There I was, still only nineteen years old, a member of a fine band, and starting out on my first big adventure.   And I had my new trumpet to take with me.   I reached over and let my hand lay on it, and felt very comfortable, and then before long I dozed off and slept most of the rest of that first day.

When we pulled up near to Baton Rouge, it was almost dark and the *Dixie Belle* had all her lights blazing so the town would know we'd come.   She was a pretty thing to see on the river at night, with her lights shining on the black water.   We "cats" (all jazz musicians from New Orleans called each other "cats" and still do) had got into our best clothes and were tuning up our instruments because we would always steam into port playing our strongest.

The people at Baton Rouge gave us a nice welcome. They knew, of course, we were coming and then they knew a lot about our orchestra, being so near to New Orleans.

We took a big party on board about eight o'clock and slow-poked up and down the river while they danced and sang and spooned out on the decks, and afterwards landed them back at the wharf along about eleven — the same as we had been doing all winter back home.

We had advertised an all-day excursion trip for the next day and had a big crowd for that, too. We started out at nine o'clock in the morning and made quite a run upriver where we tied up in pretty country for awhile so the people who wanted to could go ashore and build fires and eat the picnic lunches everybody brought along. In the afternoon, we drifted back down the river, getting in about six o'clock. Of course, we'd play for them every once in a while through the day and always showed them we were glad to play anything they particularly asked us to play. They had a wonderful time.

When we ran these all-day excursions, and we did that at most all of the ports we touched at, it only left the orchestra about two hours to rest up and get dressed and ready for the evening excursions. It was a very hard routine. Hot musicians throw a pack of energy into their work and it takes a lot out of them.

The second morning after we reached Baton Rouge we started north again. That was the morning we felt we were really starting off because Baton Rouge had been a lot like New Orleans and most of us had been there before. Our next town was a hundred miles farther up and in another state — Natchez, Mississippi.

As we went on up the river I had become more and more surprised at the way the river twisted around. If you look at it on a big map, you'll see a wavy line that looks like a ten-year-old kid writing a line of "m's" and "w's." "Steamboat 'Round the Bend," it was, most of the time — often you could only see a few miles ahead or behind. And as the current swept around those curves and corners it was sometimes a whole rush of water that the boat could hardly pull against. Also, the way it ran was always changing the channel and kicking up new sandbars or sweeping away ones that had been there a day or two before. We got stuck on sandbars several times, and one time in particular that I'll tell you about later that wasn't very much fun.

It took a mighty fine and steady captain to handle a big steamer on that powerful river, and we had one of the best of 'em on the *Dixie Belle*. He was an old hand and sure knew that old river. They said that in the thirty years or more that he had been piloting on it, he had never lost his boat, or even damaged one bad. One afternoon when he had turned the wheel over to a member of the crew for a spell, he stopped and talked a little to me. He was a wonderful old gentleman, with a white beard and bushy eyebrows and under them the keenest eyes I think I have ever seen. I knew all real Mississippi pilots were very proud of being so, as they have a mighty good right to be, so I was particularly respectful to him. When I was at the Waif's Home, Mr. Peter Davis had given me a book of Mr. Mark Twain's to read. The book was "Tom Sawyer," and I had liked it and always wanted to meet a boy like "Tom." Mr. Davis told me Mr. Twain had been a river pilot once himself and was always talking about it, so I asked our captain if he could remember him. It pleased the old man mighty to ask him and he told me, yes, when he was very young, he had known Mr. Twain and used to sit on his knee and hear him tell stories about the river and piloting, and that was one of the things that had made him decide to become a pilot when he grew up. He said before our trip was over we would pass "Jackson Island" where "Tom" and his "pirates" had had their camp. But that, he said, was more than a thousand miles upriver.

On our night excursion out of Natchez, while we were swinging some good number for the folks, the first mate came up to "Fate" Marable and said, "Can you boys play the Wedding March?" "Fate" asked us and we said we thought we could. "Well," the mate said, "make it the next number, because we're going to have a wedding on board." And sure enough, in walked a minister and a young couple who had decided it would be a romantic thing to be married out on the river on the *Dixie Belle*. So the minister married them right there in the dance salon and we swung the old wedding march for them. The mate got some rice from the galley and everybody threw it at the bride and groom and then they all made a big circle and started dancing around them and singing, "There'll be a Hot Time in the Old Town Tonight." We had joined in for all we were worth, when all of a sudden above all the noise we heard a shout that made everybody stand stock-still in their tracks. It was a deckhand singing out, "Man Overboard!" In a second there was a rush to the deck and all of the people crowded over to the port rail. It was almost too much for the *Dixie Belle*. She lurched over suddenly and I thought she was going clean over on her side. The mate dashed up to us and yelled, "Keep playing! Play hard!" We took his orders and stuck to our instruments, but it was one of the hardest things I ever did in my life. In the meantime all the officers were running through the crowd, shouting and cursing for them to stand back to the middle of the boat and very soon they had her back on an even keel and were quieting down the crowd which was pretty scared of what had happened through their all rushing to one side like that.

There was no use trying to rescue the man. A strong current had swept him way downstream by that time and it was pitch dark on the water. They threw out some life preservers but they knew it wasn't any use. The crowd had got very quiet and you could see there would be no more party that night. All of a sudden I heard an awful scream and then a woman came running through the salon calling out a man's name. I remember it was "Henry." "Henry! Henry! Henry!" she screamed, "Oh, please, Henry." But nobody in the crowd answered. It was the new bride. Some of the women ran over and got hold of her and led her away, but for a long time we could hear her sobbing and calling out. A little while later we learned the truth. The man Henry who had jumped over into the river had been engaged to marry her and the night before she had put him aside for the new groom. He had come aboard for her wedding party, but when the wedding started and everyone was inside, he had stayed out on deck alone, by the port rail. I guessed that when he heard the music and the shouting inside and knew it was all over and she was gone for good, he couldn't stand it.

As we worked on up the river, crossing and crossing back, to this town and that, we boys in the orchestra naturally got to know each other very well. We slept in the same part of the boat and had our meals at the same table and in fact we were together most all of the time. Before we reached Natchez I had made friends with a member of the band who was to do a great deal for me —almost more than anyone else besides "King" Oliver. His name was David Jones and of course everybody called him "Davey." He played a very unusual instrument called a "melophone." He was the only melophone player I have ever known. It was a brass horn with several coils and a pretty big bell. Davey could play that thing so it almost talked to you, and was he hot! He was a trained musician, too, and it was Davey who really taught me to read music. He taught me the value of a note and how to divide and how to phrase and the rest. And because he liked me and I liked him and admired him so much, both as a man and as a musi-

cian, he was able to impress upon me the importance
of knowing how to read and understand written music.
He used to say to me, "Louis, you can blow, and you
can swing because it's natural to you. But you'll never
be able to swing any better than you already know how
until you learn to read. Then you will swing in ways
you never thought of before." And he was right.
Davey Jones cared so much about my being trained better that he taught me for half an hour every afternoon
through the six more months we were on the river that
summer. And I think he will say that I gave him my
attention and learned fast. Davey finally had to give
up the melophone which he loved so much and learn
to play the saxophone, because later on the sax got very
popular with jazz orchestras and nobody knew much
about his instrument and wouldn't engage him. It was
a shame. He is doing well now as the head of a music
school back in New Orleans. And *I* know the pupils
who go to Davey Jones' school will really learn something about swing music. And I should know.

After Natchez, we went on up, about sixty miles or so,
to Vicksburg and after a couple of days there started
out again on the long two or three hundred mile stretch
to Memphis, the first really big town up above New
Orleans. On the way, we stopped for a day at Green-
ville, Mississippi, and a day at Phillips, Arkansas, on the
west shore.

Memphis was "big time" and we stayed there quite a
few days. On one of the evening excursions the boat

was chartered by the Memphis lodge of one of the fraternal organizations and they insisted on bringing their own band along with them.   This band was headed by a big brown man with a French name.   When he brought his band on board it was easy to see he had had a lot of "corn" and felt he practically owned the *Dixie Belle*. "Fate" Marable was terrible mad about it and I began to feel afraid there would be some bad trouble for us later on.   That kind of man is likely to be very quick and nasty with his knife, especially when he's drinking. I had seen plenty of that in the honky tonks in the old Third Ward.   And "Fate" was very high-strung and quick himself, although always a real gentleman who never went out of his way looking for trouble.   "Fate" had been brought up from a boy by the family which owned the boat line the *Dixie Belle* was part of, and they had given him a good education.

As it turned out, "Fate" kept his head about him and nothing serious did happen, but I was glad that night when that man and his band finally went down the gangplank.

After Memphis, we went on up about seventy-five miles to Carruthersville where we spent a day.   Across the river on the east shore was Tennessee.   Then we were off again for another seventy-five miles or so until we came into Cairo, Illinois.   Cairo was a pretty important stop.   The Ohio River came into the Mississippi there, and also three states met in a point there, Illinois, Missouri and Kentucky.   The Ohio cuts

through, and makes a boundary the same way, where
Indiana, Ohio and Kentucky come together in a point.
I remember, because I played that point on the road
some years later with "King" Oliver's band.

We ran excursions out of Cairo, day and night, for
several days, and one day we even poked up the Ohio
River as far as Paducah, Kentucky, and spent the night.

We were now about half way on our trip north and
only about a hundred and fifty miles or so south of St.
Louis which was our big stop and where we were to
spend six or seven weeks. We all looked forward to
St. Louis. We had had a hard grind of it and, with
all of the one-day stops, and playing day and evening,
had had almost no chance to leave the boat at all. We
only made one stop, as I remember, between Cairo and
St. Louis, and that was for a day and evening at Mur-
physville. But like a horse who's got his head turned
toward his stable, we didn't think much about that.
Toward evening the following day, we steamed smart
into St. Louis, lights blazing all over the boat and our
orchestra playing hot. Yeah man!

V. ST. LOUIS BLUES

WE New Orleans boys had been used to keeping very late hours, playing as we did in cabaret orchestras. We generally didn't get to bed until near to morning. So the life on the *Dixie Belle,* while it was hard work running those excursions, really had done me a lot of good. We couldn't go ashore much during the days or evenings, up to eleven o'clock at night when we pulled in. And after eleven there was no place to go. Most all of the towns we played closed up tight at that hour. So I got to going to bed earlier and getting up early.

In St. Louis, though, we knew we were headed for some night life again.

The people at St. Louis were surprised to see a colored orchestra on the *Dixie Belle.* It was the first time, as I believe I said before, that colored "cats" had ever come North to play there. The people learned to like us right away. Every night, at the top of the program "Fate" would swing us into the *St. Louis Blues* and they would go crazy about our music. It was good all right. Just a few days after we arrived, the boys in the band began to get invitations to parties in the city and some of the best players were invited to be guest performers with local bands in the big cabarets. We usually had some place to go every night when we got in from the evening trip.

On July 4th, I was twenty years old, and the boys gave me a little birthday party in the city. It's nice having a birthday on a holiday, if it isn't Christmas.

One night "Fate" and Davey Jones and I were invited to be special guests at one of the most famous places in town. I cannot remember the name of it, but it was a big place and crowded with people. The leader of the orchestra was a good musician and interested in everything that was happening in jazz. He had kept in touch as much as he could with the progress of jazz in New Orleans and when "Fate" and Davey and I arrived he treated us very nice and was very respectful to us. He said he hoped we would sit down and have a little drink with him later on, so we could talk. Before that, however, he said, he hoped we three would take a number alone and "show us St. Louisians how they swing in New Orleans." I was younger than "Fate" Marable and a lot younger than Davey Jones and I was mighty proud indeed to be in their company that night and to be included with them.

We three sat to one side of the band and listened to them play. We could see the boys in the band had heard about us. They kept looking over at us, in a curious way, but not letting on they were. We watched close to see what their music would be like, because we knew they had a big reputation in St. Louis, and naturally we were interested to see how our New Orleans bands, like Kid Ory's and the rest, would stack up against them. Well, we were surprised. In no time at all we could tell they were doing things that had been done down home years before. The leader would try to swing them away from the score but they didn't seem to know how. I thought I could see he knew what we were thinking, because every once in a while he would look over to us and smile, but not as if he were sure we were liking it. After several numbers he had his trumpeter do a call to attention. When the room was quiet, he stepped out in front and announced: "We are honored to have with us tonight three of New Orleans' most distinguished performers. They come from the town where they even have jazz music with their breakfast. And need I say more than that they come from the home port of the 'Dixieland Band.' They have kindly consented to play a number for us and will show us how they swing that music down in old New Orleans. Ladies and Gentlemen, let me present Mr. 'Fate' Marable, at the piano, Mr. David Jones, on the melophone, and Mr. Louis Armstrong, on the trumpet."

When we took our places we got a big hand. We were glad to be on shore again and very set up over the fine introduction we had had, so we were feeling high. It wasn't easy to handle a number with just a piano and two "brasses," but Davey and I had figured out a plan we thought would work. We cut loose with one of the very newest hot songs that had just been getting around home when we left — and we let it swing, plenty. Every one of us three was a natural swing player and didn't need any scoring at all. We almost split that room

open — man, did we play! I got so hot I hardly knew
there was a room. Davey threw that big horn of his
around so you'd have thought he'd gone clean out of
his head, and "Fate" kept right along with us. Boy!
Could "Fate" make those keys sing! Well, they all
liked it fine. They stood up and yelled out for more
and the band boys were all on their feet, too, and the
leader came over and shook our hands. We gave them
an encore and then, as a courtesy to them, we played
the *St. Louis Blues* the way we had swung it back
home. My, that was a big night for me. I will never
forget it. It was the first time I had had an ovation
like that in a really big city away from New Orleans. I
don't mean to say I took it all to myself, but just that I
was part of it. It was long after two o'clock before the
leader was free and then we four went back to his dressing room and sat down around a table. We all liked
him a lot, and he had been very nice to us. He asked us
about Kid Ory and about Perez and others he knew
about and we told him everything we could. Then he
started talking about Chicago, which was nearer to St.
Louis than New Orleans was, and remarked that "King"
Oliver was making a big hit at the Lincoln Gardens.
My, I was glad to hear "Papa Joe" was doing so well,
though I always had the greatest confidence in him,
because he was my real hero.

The *Dixie Belle* ran daily excursions out of St. Louis
for six weeks that summer. Some days we would go

as far as Alton, Illinois, and thereabouts. But it was beginning to tell on me, staying up to late hours and having to be back on the boat, ready to start out on the day trip at nine o'clock every morning, not to mention playing all day long and again on the evening trip. So when the time finally came for us to leave for the North, I was dogged out, and not sorry we were going. Our next big stop was to be St. Paul. That was five hundred miles away.

After we got out on the river again I began to get rested up. The summer was pretty well along, so we steamed upstream on many days without stopping anywhere, passing by all the towns we knew weren't good "show towns." I had a chance to laze around the decks in the daytime and get sleep at night. While we were in St. Louis I had forgotten about my own troubles, but now, when I was rested up and quiet again, I began to think about Daisy and wish I were with her. I told myself I needed her and she needed me.

It was getting on late in August and we were hoping to make St. Paul in time for the Labor Day holiday when we would have big crowds. The weather was terribly hot. You couldn't get cool anywhere; it was just as hot inside the boat as up on deck. We boys and some of the deck-hands got half a dozen long ropes and fixed big loops on the ends and threw them out over the stern, making the other ends fast along the rail. Then we took hold of the ropes and let ourselves out into the water until we got down to the loops, which we would slip around under our arms, and lay back and let the boat pull us along. It didn't help much because the river water was almost hot to touch. The mate soon stopped that. He said if a snag or piece of plank should come along we'd have our bellies ripped out of us.

It got so hot that one night I couldn't sleep at all, and that is something very unusual for me because I sure can tear off my sleep. I can sleep any old time and anywhere I get the chance. But not that night. After awhile I got up and went out on deck, hoping to get some cool air. The *Dixie Belle* was moving along in almost pitch dark, her paddles making a soft, chunking sound. I could see a few stars high up overhead. I found my old corner and sat down. Above the beat of the paddles, everything was still. The shore seemed a long way off. I could just make it out, going past very slow, like a black wall. I sat and watched it. Pretty soon I began to feel alone, and looked around me. There was nothing but the darkness and the steady plunk, plunk of the wheels. I felt far off and not there where I was. I put my hands down on the deck and let them run over the planks, to feel them under me. After a little while I got quiet and began to take comfort out of the stillness, and didn't mind being alone. I thought again about my little wife. I knew I loved her. I made up my mind that the troubles we had gone through had been mostly my own fault, and I decided, then and there, that if she would only wait for me to come back, I would make her happy.

We steamed up and up the river. Late one evening one of the mates stopped short in front of me where I was sitting on the after-deck and said, "Armstrong, the captain wants you at once in the pilot house." I was a little worried, wondering if I had done something he hadn't liked. I followed the mate. He led me along to the companionway, which is the stairway going up to the next deck. He went up smart, rat, tat, tat, and I followed on up after him. When he got to the pilot house he knocked on the door and when the captain opened, he touched his cap and said, "Here is Armstrong, sir," and turned and left me. I looked up at the old gentleman, not knowing what was to come. Then I saw he was smiling. He said, "Louie, come in here. We're working up to Jackson Island in a few minutes and I thought you would like to see it." He had remembered my telling him about my reading "Tom Sawyer" and asking him if he had known Mr. Mark Twain.

He stood there behind the pilot wheel with his big strong hand ahold of one of the spokes. He had me stand up to the wheel beside him, and lay his other hand on my shoulder. It felt heavy and kind. The *Dixie Belle* was ploughing on. He was quiet for a time, looking out over the dark water ahead, and I got a feeling that he had forgotten I was there. Pretty soon he said, "This is Mark Twain's country. He was a very great man. I never pass this part of the river without feeling that his spirit rests over it."

Before long, I noticed the wheel was turning to the

right, and soon I began to see a dark patch of woods
standing out ahead of us on the left. Then I heard
his voice again. "That is Jackson Island," the old gentleman said. I knew the time had come when I should
feel something he wanted me to feel. I remembered
from the book about how Tom Sawyer and Huckleberry
Finn and their friend little Joe Harper had gone to that
island to be "pirates," and had cooked their food over a
wood fire and had had a good time, but that seemed a
long way back to me, and the island, as far as I could see
it in the dark, looked just the same as a hundred other
islands we had passed in the river in the long time we had
been going since we left New Orleans.

VI. *STORMY WEATHER*

THE next day after that we came up to Quincy, Illinois, and decided to stop a day.   That is what we never should have done, though nobody could have known it ahead of time.

The river had been falling and the *Dixie Belle* had to keep very close to the channel where it was deep enough, for she was a pretty big boat.   I noticed the captain didn't leave the pilot house very often.   One of the older deck-hands, who had been working on the river boats since he was a boy, said he didn't believe he could remember seeing so many sandbars before.

Quincy wasn't more than a hundred miles north of St. Louis, if that far, and the people had heard about our orchestra making a hit in St. Louis and were waiting for us.   One of their local brass bands came down to the wharf and played us in, which was very nice of them. I think musicians everywhere are pretty much that way to each other.

That evening we took out a big crowd for a moonlight sail up the river.   We pulled out into the channel, swinging *Tiger Rag,* about nine o'clock.   I noticed it was beginning to cloud up a little back of the town. We went up the river quite a piece.   Along about ten o'clock people came hurrying in from the decks, the

men with their coat collars up and the girls with coats
or wraps thrown over their hair.   One old lady had
lifted the back of her dress clean up over her head and
came running in in her petticoat.   There had been a
cloudburst and it had come up quick and caught them.
My, how that rain did rain !   A great roaring of wind
came with it.   Things began banging about all over the
boat.   A lot of camp-stools the excursionists had brought
on board were sliding back and forth across the after-
deck, making a terrible racket.   The *Dixie Belle* was
hit hard and was rolling and pitching around bad.
Every few minutes, through the storm, I could hear far
off the clank, clank of the gong down in the engine room.
I knew the engineer was getting signals from the pilot
house, and that the old gentleman was fighting to hold
the *Dixie Belle* to the channel.   I felt glad he was up
there, with his strong old hands on the *Dixie Belle's*
wheel.

All of the people were crowded inside and the dance
salon was jammed.   It soon got hot and close with the
windows shut down.   After a few minutes, somebody
called for music and they started dancing again, thinking
it was fun to dance in the storm.   When the boat would
roll over to one side, they'd slide down the floor and
pile all up, laughing.   Then down they'd slide the other
way.   Before long I heard loud clanging in the engine
room and then shouts outside, and it was only a few
seconds after that, it seemed, before there was an awful
bump.   The *Dixie Belle* shook all over, and then began

plunging up and down like a bucking horse. I heard the machinery come to a sudden stop, then start up again — I knew the paddles had gone into reverse, trying to pull us backward off the bar.

People were picking themselves up off the floor where they had been thrown and were bunching together. Somebody yelled out that the boat was sinking. "Fate" shouted to us, "Let's play!" Most of our chairs and instrument racks were upset and sliding around so we went into a fast number, standing up. It helped to quiet them. In a few minutes one of the outside doors opened and two of the mates came in. They had to put their shoulders hard to the door to get it closed, the wind was rushing in so strong. Everybody went toward them. The mates were very calm and said there was no cause for alarm, that the *Dixie Belle* had run onto a sandbar but they hoped to have her off soon. They said the boat was good and sound and was not taking any water, and that if the worst came to the worst there were plenty of life-boats and the nearest shore was only half a mile away. They said the life-boats were all ready, if they should be needed, and in the meantime the crew would pass out life preservers, so everyone would have one. Then they asked everybody if they would be calm and have confidence in the captain.

When the crowd heard this they acted pretty fine, I will say. The men helped the girls put on the life preservers and some of the young people started dancing around in them, playful, and that made the others laugh

and put them in better spirits. I could tell from the
way we kept bouncing up and down that the bow of the
Dixie Belle was fast on the bar with the stern free in
deeper water. After quite a while, it must have been
well on to midnight by that time, the mates came in
again and said the storm was beginning to let up,
but that it looked as though they wouldn't be able to
get back to Quincy before morning. They advised
everybody to make themselves as comfortable as possible
and said that hot coffee and sandwiches were being fixed
in the galley and would be passed out. They came over
to Marable and asked him if we would stay on duty and
play anything the crowd wanted, to keep them in good
humor. Very soon after that, almost as suddenly as it
had started, the storm stopped. We opened up the windows and got some cool air. The people had coffee and
we played a little more for them, and then they began to
get comfortable so they could get a little sleep. The
women lay down on the benches that went around the
sides of the salon, and the men put chairs together for
themselves or lay on the floor. Everybody was dog-tired
out. When we saw they didn't want any more music,
we closed up and went down to our own rooms. There
we learned from some of the deckhands what had happened. The *Dixie Belle* had broken a rudder chain
in the storm and with the rudder smashing around had
gone head-on onto a big bar, and was stuck fast. They
said it was no use trying to get her off the bar until the
rudder could be fixed, and that might take another whole

day. Then they could probably work her off the bar and get the people back to Quincy. Outside of the rudder, they said, the boat was all right and as good as ever.

The next day came up bright and nice, and the river quiet. You'd never have thought there had been a storm. When I went up into the dance salon, coffee and corn-bread and plates of hot boiled rice were being passed around. The *Dixie Belle* didn't carry enough fresh food for a crowd like that, only enough for the officers and crew and the orchestra, but there was plenty of coffee and cornmeal and flour and beans and rice and that kind of food on hand. All of us were asked to help out fixing or carrying up the breakfast for the excursionists. It looked funny to see them all in their party clothes in the morning. All the combs that were on board were in great demand and were being passed around from one to another. They were pretty good-natured, but I guess they'd had a hard night and I felt real sorry for them.

The time we lost at Quincy made us late getting into St. Paul in time for Labor Day, because we lost three whole days more. Towards the end of the next day, after the storm, we got the rudder fixed up enough to take a chance on getting back to the town, with the river calm, and right away started working off the bar. The paddles would drive us forward, and then reverse, and then forward again and reverse, until finally, after a couple of hours, we edged off into good deep water.

Everybody cheered, and we slid out into the channel and headed for Quincy.

By the time we got in sight of the town it was dark. We could see the wharf was lighted up and crowded with people. The whole town had been afraid the *Dixie Belle* had been lost in the storm, and watch had been kept, and lights played on the water all the night before. After we had landed the people, we tied up for the night. Some new part was needed for the rudder before we dared go on and possibly get into another storm like that one, and we had to send way back to St. Louis to get what was needed.

While we were waiting around for that, I spent two evenings in the town and on the first night met a little colored girl who was in high school. She liked my music a lot and was very nice to me. We had a real good time together and I wonder if she remembers it now. We sure fried some fish those two nights.

Well, the *Dixie Belle* was fixed the next morning after, and we steamed out of Quincy early and turned upstream again. We still had four hundred miles to St. Paul. We went right on up past Keokuk and Burlington, Iowa, and Davenport, Dubuque and Winona, hoping to make up time. Day after day the orchestra didn't have anything to do at all, except "Fate" would have us rehearse once in a while. I spent a lot of time with Davey Jones and learned reading better and better. Davey would take his melophone and have me take my trumpet and we would find a quiet place on deck and he'd work with me. He would show me a passage written down and explain it to me and tell me what I should do with it, and then he would carry the melody on his melophone and I would follow him with the trumpet.

Finally, on Labor Day night, we pulled up to St. Paul. It was too late. We stayed there a few days, running excursions, but the weather was cool for river parties and business was not good. So the *Dixie Belle* got on coal and stocked up and started the long trip down to New Orleans. I was mighty glad when we were headed downstream at last. I had had a wonderful time, and many experiences, but it had been my first trip away from home and I was longing to be back. I was truly homesick. I wanted to see Daisy, and my mother and "Mamma Lucy," and Kid Ory and my old friends. We picked up Davenport and Burlington, and Keokuk, on the way down, but passed by Quincy. As we went on past, I thought of my little high school girl and wished we had stopped.

At St. Louis we pulled in and spent another good week. After that the excursion season was getting along late, so we headed pretty straight down river for New Orleans, making stops only at big towns like Cairo and Memphis and Vicksburg and a few others. When we got way down, drawing closer to the delta, we played again at Natchez and at Baton Rouge. The next day after that we were due to come into our old wharf at the foot of Canal Street. That last day was a long day for all of us but it did go past, and along about four o'clock

in the afternoon we came in sight of the city. All of us
were out on deck. My, we were glad to know we were
almost home! The *Dixie Belle* got on down alongside
her dock and then worked on into her old wharf, and
ticd up. My mother and "Mamma Lucy" were there,
as I was sure they'd be, waiting for me when I came off.
I was so glad to see them I couldn't tell them. They
cried a little, and my mother held me off from her and
looked at me up and down and said, "My 'Little Louie' is
grown up."

But Daisy wasn't there. As soon as I thought I could,
I asked my mother how Daisy was, and said I had hoped
she would come to meet me, too. My mother said, "Son,
I am sure your wife wants to see you, and as much as
Lucy and I want you to come home with us, I think you
had better go to her."

VII. *WITH "KING" OLIVER ON THE SOUTH SIDE*

THAT winter passed the same as the winter before, playing in Marable's orchestra and running excursions out from Canal Street. Then April came around and I decided to go north with the *Dixie Belle* for another summer. For several weeks after I had come home, Daisy and I were happy together and then our troubles began all over again the way they were before. We just couldn't seem to keep things quiet and smooth between us — there was always something coming up to spoil it. It was a shame.

The trip up river that second summer, the summer of 1921, was like the first, except that we played at a few new towns and skipped some we had visited before. I was sorry Quincy was one of those we skipped. I guess the captain didn't feel any too good about that place. We had another long stay at St. Louis where I saw the friends I had made the year before, and then we went up and caught St. Paul in good time for Labor Day.

Getting home the second time wasn't as big a kick as the first time, of course, but I am always glad to be back in New Orleans, at any time.

I had played on the boat for two full years by then, and travelled about five thousand miles in all. Playing and practising day and night, and the experience of playing to hundreds of crowds, had done a lot for me. I could read music very well by now and was getting hotter and hotter on my trumpet. My chest had filled out deeper and my lips and jaws had got stronger, so I could blow much harder and longer than before without getting tired. I had made a special point of the high register, and was beginning to make my high-C notes more and more often. That is the greatest strain on the lips. Even today I am very careful about my lips, because if a trumpeter's lips go back on him, he's just done.

But I was getting tired of the routine on the boat and ready for a change, so I decided to join the orchestra at Tom Anderson's cabaret. They featured me in trumpet solos. On the side, I joined up with the "Tuxedo" marching brass band.

Daisy and I couldn't get along any better than before. We were running into our fourth year of marriage, so we decided to get a divorce.

Winter and spring of 1922 went by. I was doing very well with my music. Along in July, just after my twenty-second birthday, the Tuxedo Band was called out one day to march in a fraternal funeral. It was terribly hot out on the street and I remember my uniform almost choked me. After the lodge member was buried, we marched on back to the lodge house. As we were disbanding somebody came up with a telegram. It was for me. I couldn't imagine what it could be. I opened it and found it was from "King" Oliver. It said he had

a place for me in his band and wanted me to come at
once to Chicago. "Papa Joe" had meant what he said.

A few days later, my mother and her husband, my
step-daddy, and "Mamma Lucy" and some of my best
friends went down to the train to see me go.   It was the
last time I was to see New Orleans again for nine years,
and the last time I was ever to see my mother until I saw
her on her death-bed, for she died very young—in her
early forties.

Well, we pulled into the old LaSalle Street station in
Chicago about ten o'clock at night.   I went right over
with my bag to the Lincoln Gardens, which was at
Thirty-first and Gordon Streets.   When I walked in the
door, "King" Oliver was standing out there in front of
his orchestra, swinging away.   It was a big place, with a
big balcony all around, and I felt a little frightened, and
wondered how I was going to make out.   I knew it was
such a big chance for me.   I went on up to the bandstand and there were some of the boys I had known back
home.   They were glad to see me and I was tickled to
death to see them all.   The band was the hit of Chicago
at that time, but as you know that was a good many years
ago.   It was made up as follows: "King" Oliver, ace
trumpet ; "Baby" Dodds, drums ; Honoré Dutrey, trombone ; Johnnie Dodds, clarinet ; Bill Johnson, bass violin,
a piano, and a second trumpet, the place I had come to
take.   Bill Johnson had gone north some years before
with the old pioneer "Creole Jazz Band."

Of course I couldn't start in playing with them that night — I needed to rehearse with them a little and get onto their ways. I went in the next week. That first night "Papa Joe" was very kind to me. He said he was going to take me home with him and that I should live with him for a while until I got more used to Chicago. His wife Stella was a very fine lady and they had a daughter named Ruby who is married now. "Mamma Stella" was a good cook and used to feed me up. That is when I began to take on weight, trying to keep up with "Papa Joe" in eating.

One night soon after I started in, and after our show was over "Papa Joe" said to me, "Louis, do you want to go over and meet Lil? She's playing at the 'Dreamland' now." I knew who he meant. The winter before "King" Oliver had sent a picture of his band down to New Orleans and the pianist in the band was an attractive looking, brown-skinned girl named Lillian Hardin. I had said in my next letter to him, "Tell Miss Lil I like her." I certainly never thought anything would come of it. So I was a little bit embarrassed when "Papa Joe" mentioned it, but I said I didn't care if I went with him.

The "Dreamland" was a very popular night-club. They had a fine band, too, headed by Ollie Powers, a great entertainer and singer. He used to be a partner of Sheldon Brooks. Ollie was a good friend to me later. When we got there Lillian Hardin was at the piano. She was, and is, one of the best woman jazz pianists in the country. "King" Oliver introduced us. He didn't know, or maybe he *did* have an idea, that he was introducing me to my second wife.

After that first night I didn't see much of Lil for two or three months, until she came back to join our band at the Lincoln Gardens. Pretty soon we got to going around more and more together. Lil believed in me from the first. Being new in a big town and not sure I could make good, her believing in me meant a great deal and helped me a lot. She told me one night she thought I could swing trumpet better than "King" Oliver and said I should have a chance to be first trumpet myself, and would never get it as long as I stayed with "Papa Joe's" band, because, naturally, he was first trumpet with his own band. I knew she was talking big, and just laughed at her. But I could see, too, that she was serious and thinking of me. Lil had been born in Memphis, but she had lived in Chicago a long time where she had studied music. She was always going to music school to learn more about it, and she studies that way still. We used to practise together, "wood-shed" as we say (from the old-time way of going out into the wood-shed to practise a new song). She would play on the piano and I, of course, on my trumpet. I had learned how to transpose from a piano part. We used to play classical music together sometimes. We bought classical trumpet music. Through this, later on, we played in churches once in a while. All of this was giving me more and more knowledge of my music.

Right here I want to say something more about swing

music, because this book isn't supposed to be so much
about me as about swing; where it came from, how it
grew and what it is.   It is just an accident that swing and
I were born and brought up side by side in New Orleans,
travelled up the Mississippi together, and, in 1922, the
year I am writing about now, were there in Chicago
getting acquainted with the North — and the North getting acquainted with us.

When you're brought up with something and it has
been natural to you, you may love it, but you don't
ever appreciate it — you can't, because you haven't meas-
ured it against anything else.   Maybe it's good, and
maybe it's bad, but you'll never really know until you
put it against something else like it.   Well, as I began
to see soon after I got around a little in Chicago, I had
been swimming all my life in a pond with a lot of real
big fish.   I had been brought up with a group of great
musicians.   They didn't know Bach from Beethoven, or
Mozart from Mendelssohn, and maybe hadn't even heard
of them, and, strange as it may sound, I think that is
exactly why they became great musicians.   Not knowing
much classical music, and not many of them having
proper education in reading music of any kind, they just
went ahead and made up their own music.   Before long,
and without really knowing it themselves, they had
created a brand new music, they created swing.   They
made a music for themselves which truly expressed what
they felt.   They were composers *and* players, all in one,
and they composed as they played and held what they

had done only in their musical memory. They didn't write much of it down — swing *can* be written down by someone listening to it, but if the players continue to follow it the way it is written down, very soon swing becomes set and regular and then it is not swing any more and that is what almost happened later when jazz tunes became so popular. People began writing them down and publishing them and wanted to have them played the way they were written. Swing music, as it started in New Orleans, was almost wiped out. Only because a few men really loved it and held onto it, it came through, and only in the last few years has the true swing come back to its own, the way it started out. The very soul and spirit of swing music is free improvisation, or "swinging" by the player.

If those early swing musicians had gone to music schools and been taught to know and worship the great masters of classical music and been told it was sacrilegious to change a single note of what was put before them to play, swing music would never have been born at all. They would have got the idea that written music, whether it is a great classic or just a popular air, is something sacred that must never be touched, especially by a beginner. That was the way music was tought in the schools, and nobody ever questioned it. Every piece of music, good or bad or indifferent, as soon as it was published was supposed to have sort of a life of its own, apart from who played it or what the player felt in playing it — and nobody could meddle with it in the least. It makes me think of the people who collect books, as against the people who write them. The book-collector gets to feel that a book has a life of its own and is sacred, apart from what's in it, and just because it is written down and bound up in covers.

Now I do not believe that books or music, or any other kind of art, are sacred, or even important to us, apart from what they truly express. What makes a composer or author or artist a real master is that his work so wonderfully expressed what he felt that nobody but a clumsy fool would *want* to change it. As likely as not he didn't follow after anybody else's way of doing, but went on his own way, as he himself felt and thought, and that is the way new and younger people should do, too, because that is the way music and art grow and the only way they can keep growing. Now I think that there are two kinds of men chiefly who *can* break loose like that. One is the kind of man who learns everything about his art and what has been done before him so he can go on beyond it, and the other is the kind who doesn't know *anything* about it — who is just plain ignorant, but has a great deal of feeling he's got to express in some way, and has to find that way out for himself. Swing came mostly from the last kind of men. That is why, during those early years, people noticed two things about it, that it was very strong and vital, and also that it was crude and not "finished." And it is very true that the swing music we have today is far more refined and subtle and more highly developed as an art because the swing

men who learned to read and understand classical music
have brought classical influences into it. I think that
may be said to be the real difference between the original
New Orleans "jazz" and the swing music of today. And
in taking in the classical influence, real jazz has gained
a very great deal and not lost — it is growing into a finer
and broader and richer music, a music that is truly American, that will surely take its place, in time, alongside
of the great and permanent music of other countries.
Until swing music came, America had no music it could
really call its own. If you will look at the European
music journals, you will see what their critics think of
our own swing music. You will see that they already
think of it as a new and permanent music. Some of
them even write that the swing principle of free improvisation by the player will affect all of music — and
at last make the player, the instrumentalist, as important as the composer, because he, too, in swing, becomes a composer — a player-composer. I don't know
about that, but it is funny that swing music got its first
serious recognition, not at home, but in Europe. During my own three years playing in England and on the
Continent, the very finest music critics would come back
to my dressing room, or call upon me at my hotel, and
talk with me for hours about the "significance" of our
music and what they thought it meant. That had never
happened to me before, in America, although since I
have been home this last time I notice that our own
critics and journals are beginning to have the same kind

of serious interest.   I don't believe that I, myself, ever
realized swing music was really important until I went
to Europe and saw what they thought of it.   I had just
been playing it and growing with it since I was a kid.

Well, to go back to the winter of 1922-1923, the first
winter I was in Chicago when swing was hot as fire but
still pretty crude in form.   I had only been there a little
while, as I said, before I began to see how much I had
learned in the South.   There were only a very few bands
that played the way we did, and most of the good players,
though not all of them, had come North from the lower
Mississippi country, from Memphis down to the delta.
Another thing I noticed quickly was that the people who
liked those bands best at that time, and followed them,
were the people who didn't know much about the older
music, mostly the young people in highschools and colleges.   They loved to hear us swing, and to dance to it.
Then there were a few real musicians, classical musicians,
who liked us.   There was a professor of music in one of
the big Chicago colleges who used to come down to the
Lincoln Gardens and sit there night after night, taking
notes.   The waiters didn't like him much because he
never ordered a drink and never brought anybody with
him, but just sat there and listened.   I didn't understand
it then, but I do now.   As I say, it is the very learned
man or the very ignorant one who can break loose, and I
say, too, about most of the musical people of that day, and
a lot of them still today, "there's none so blind as he who

will not see." But swing has gone on anyway, and will go on. The men who play it and make it put their music ahead of everything in their lives.

Take the "jam sessions" for instance. I am sure you have heard about them. Where do you find anything like that among "regular" or "sweet" musicians? A group of swing players, tired out after their pay performances, getting together alone in the early morning hours to swing together just for the fun of it. "Swing it, Gate," one of them will sing out and that will be a "sender" to them and they'll all go into their music, swinging hot, only because they love it. That "sender," "Swing it, Gate," by the way, came from me. When I was a kid, you remember, they started calling me "Gate-mouth," and then "Satchel-mouth." Well, I started calling the other boys "Gate," too, to sort of throw it back at them, so it wouldn't stick too close to me, I guess. Then I got used to saying it and when I got into Kid Ory's band when the boys were all swinging good and hot, I would sing out, "Swing it, Gate." That has stuck to me ever since, like "Satchmo," and now "Gate" is a word swing players use when they call out to one another in their own language, but most of them, I guess, don't know how it started. I have heard some of them explain that it came from the word "alligator" — that is the word we use for a person who is not a player himself but who loves to sit and listen to swing music. We will say about some new number we plan to play, "The 'alligators' will like that." I may mention here that there are more than four hundred words used among swing musicians that no one else would understand. They have a language of their own, and I don't think anything could show better how closely they have worked together and how much they feel that they are apart from "regular" musicians and have a world of their own that they believe in and that most people have not understood. I hope this book will help to explain it a little — it is the real reason I have tried to write it and kept on after I found out what hard-going writing was for a man who has lived all of his life mostly with a trumpet, not a pencil, in his hand.

VIII.   *TO BROADWAY WITH FLETCHER HENDERSON*

In April 1923, when our winter engagement at the Lincoln Gardens was over, "King" Oliver took us on a road trip down through Illinois and Ohio and Indiana, playing one-night stands in ball-rooms.   It was a nice trip. We stopped at Richmond, Indiana, to make some phonograph recordings for the Gennett Company.   It was my first experience making records, though I have made enough of them since, a great many of my best ones for "Decca."   Some of "King" Oliver's Gennett records of those days are very valuable today and are collected by those who study the evolution of swing music.   I think it was then that I realized for the first time how strong my blowing had become with all those years of practising and playing.   The Gennett people found they had to put me twenty feet back of the other players because my high-register notes were so strong they would not record clearly any closer.   Lil went with us on that trip and she and I got closer and closer and less than a year later, on February 5, 1924, we were married at the City Hall in Chicago.

Lil kept on talking to Ollie Powers about me and finally Ollie offered to take me in at the "Dreamland" as first trumpet.   So I went, and it wasn't long after that, in October, that I heard again from Fletcher Henderson in New York.   He told me he had another opening for me and hoped I'd come, and this time, five years after he first asked me, I did.   Lil and I packed up and went to New York.   It was our first trip there and we had a big kick out of going, I can tell you.   As it turned out Lil could only stay a couple of weeks.   Her mother was taken very ill and she had to go back to Chicago.   I was away a year.

Fletcher had a fine twelve-piece band at the big Rose-land Ballroom which is at the corner of Broadway and 51st Street, New York.   It was the first colored dance band to play special arrangements, and what a band! We played on one bandstand and Sam Lanin's band was on the other.   Those were the days when "Red" Nichols and "Miff" Mole and Swan and Victor D'Oppolito were coming up fast, along with other musicians who are famous today.   Those boys were always nice to me.

Out on the South Side, in Chicago, I was beginning to "feel my oats" and think I was pretty good, especially when I got to be first trumpet at the "Dreamland" and then, more than ever, when Fletcher Henderson called me to come to New York.   I could blow, all right, but I hadn't counted on New York.   In that big town I was just a little small-town boy, and nobody much on Broad-way had ever heard of me.   But Harlem saved my life. They already knew a little something about me.   I had heard talk of Harlem since I was a kid, and I had always wondered what kind of place it was.   I knew it was somewhere in New York and that it was "the biggest negro city in the world." When I joined the "Roseland" band, I started living in Harlem, which is just north of Central Park in Manhattan, and began finding out what it was like. I found it had all kinds, like any big city. It had no-good floaters from all over the country, and it had thousands and thousands of good, hardworking colored people, and on top of that the most brilliant and talented musicians and actors and poets and artists of our race, mixing there together — they had come from everywhere to Harlem, which is the capital city and the city where most of our colored genius today is to be found, more than in all other places in the world, as I know. There was Charles Gilpin, the great actor in "The Emperor Jones," and Florence Mills, both dead now, and Paul Robeson and Ethel Waters and Bill Robinson and Duke Ellington and Cab Calloway and Chick Webb and James Weldon Johnson, our great poet, and those fine people who later went into the cast of "The Green Pastures" and carried that beautiful play all over the United States for five years, and many others whom I should mention.

Well, as I say, Harlem had heard a little bit about me because many of the New Orleans musicians I had known had drifted up there, and then, too, they knew about "King" Oliver's Band in Chicago and had heard me on his records. So one night when I was especially feeling how big New York was and how little I was, I was asked to do a trumpet solo at the Savoy Dance Hall, which is

Harlem's biggest and finest ballroom. Was I proud! When I went out in front in that hall, which is a whole block long, and raised up my trumpet, I got a nice big hand. My, it made me feel good to think I was not all alone, especially since I had just begun to be so set up about myself. I played my very best and they liked it so well they asked me to come a second night. That was big news for "Little Louie." But it didn't make any noise on Broadway. I had to wait five more years for that — until I came back to New York the second time.

Fletcher's band played at the "Roseland" all that winter. In April of 1925, he booked the band for a long road tour through New England and down into the mining towns of Pennsylvania. We stayed out all summer. We had the largest colored band on the road in the North and we had a big welcome wherever we went. I now played a feature trumpet. One night we happened to be playing for a big dance in Lawrence, Massachusetts, given by the local Elks Lodge. They had had a beauty contest and that night the winner of it was there. She had won a free trip to Hollywood and a chance to try out for the movies. The girl was Miss Thelma Todd who later came to a tragic death in Hollywood. When I read of it, I remembered how happy she was that night in Lawrence, with all the world, as she must have thought, right ahead of her and nothing to do but take it. All show-people have lots of trouble in their lives, I think.

We played one-night stands for many months that summer, and played opposite most of the best white bands, which, like us, had gone out from New York on the road after the close of the big winter season. I had some more wonderful experience (there is not any experience quite as good as playing on the road, as any old showman will tell you) but before it was over I began to get very homesick for Chicago and wanted to see Lil again. So when we finally came in from that tour, I told Fletcher I wanted to go back to Chicago. He had been mighty good to me and in that year I had learned a great deal.

Lil was now the pianist-leader of the "Dreamland" band, and she had me come in as featured trumpet. There were eight pieces. I was happy to be back on the South Side. Lil and I were making real good money between us and we began to do what we wanted. We bought a house and a little car and then we bought some lots on the lake-front at Idlewild, which was a summer resort on Idlewild Lake, out from Chicago. I used to like to go to Idlewild with Lil. I like to swim and hadn't had much of a chance to since I was on the Mississippi. The lake there was about a mile across and I could make that easy. But Lil wouldn't go swimming with me. I had ducked her in the water just for fun when we had spent a day once on Lake Michigan, and I guess I must have scared her too bad, without meaning to. Anyway, she wouldn't go out after that. When the crowd would go canoeing in the evenings, and sing together, she wouldn't go either. I guess some people are just naturally afraid of the water.   Another thing I liked to do was to ride horseback there. I would rent myself a good old nag for an hour or two and climb on without any saddle and in my bathing suit and ride around the country.   The weekends I could get off we went to Idlewild and this was the most exercise, and the best, I remember — although you might say blowing a trumpet is exercise all of the time.

Early in 1926, Professor Erskine Tate started talking to me about joining his little symphony orchestra at the Vendome Theatre and before long I did and stayed with Erskine for a year.   That was a good thing for me because it made me better known.   It was at the Vendome that I got to know that great swing piano player, Earl Hines.   Earl could swing a gang of keys.   He and I liked each other from the first and were to see a lot of each other afterwards.   A few months after I went to the Vendome, another big break came along for me. Earl and I were asked to double, after the theatre closed for the night, at the Sunset Cabaret, which then was one of the smartest and most popular night clubs on the South Side.   The band leader there was Carrol Dickerson, and I was to see more of him later, too.

It was at the Sunset, for the first time, that my name went up in lights.   I will never forget the kick I got when I first saw that big bright sign reading: "Louis Armstrong, World's Greatest Trumpet Player." I couldn't help thinking I had travelled pretty far since I'd left the Waif's Home, a little more than ten years before.   Mr. Joe Glaser was proprietor of the Sunset at that time.   He was the first to give me a real big play, and he is my manager today.

Several months later Carroll Dickerson's band left the Sunset and I took his place and organized my own band — twelve pieces, with two pianos, and the first big band of my own.   I surely began to work hard then, starting in at seven o'clock every night at the Vendome, then going to the Sunset and working through to three and four in the morning, rehearsing, planning new arrangements and all of that.   Also I got together a little group of swing players which were called "Louis Armstrong's Hot Five" and began to make records.   I don't know how I stood it.   I never had any time to be at home, except just for a few hours' sleep.   I met myself coming and going.   I guess it was about that time, and because of that, that Lil and I first started to drift apart, although we didn't see it then and it wasn't until 1932 that we were finally separated.

Some of those early records we made were: *Gut Bucket Blues, Butter-and-Egg Man* and *Heebie-Jeebies. Heebie-Jeebies* sold forty thousand in a few weeks and the others did about the same.   It was the time of the "Charleston" dance craze.

That year I lost my mother, Mary-Ann.   As soon as I heard she was sick I sent Lil to New Orleans to bring her to Chicago.   I kept her in the hospital three months but it was no use.   I tell you I felt bad to see her go — she had always done so much for me and loved me so and I was beginning to be able to give her what she needed and planning to see she had a nice comfortable old age. "Mamma Lucy" took it terribly hard.

When we closed our engagement at the Sunset Cabaret early in 1928, I went to the Metropolitan Theatre with Clarence Jones' orchestra. Jones is a wonderful musician. He is now with the Southern Airs Quartet on the radio. I was featured at the Metropolitan for three or four months when Carroll Dickerson, who now had his band at the Savoy Dance Hall across the street, offered me more money to join him and I did. My name was up in lights all of the time now. The collegians all liked to hear me and dance to my playing. I was getting to be a "big man" on the South Side.

IX. *"AIN'T MISBEHAVIN'"* SENDS ME

WE had a fine band now at the Savoy. We had Zutti, my old friend, up from New Orleans, handling the drums, and then we had Crawford Worthington at first alto sax, Homer Hobson, second trumpet, Fred Robinson, trombone, Gene Anderson, piano, Jimmy Strong, tenor sax, Bernard Curry, third alto sax, Peter Briggs, bass tuba, Mancy Carr, banjo, and Carroll Dickerson. I was featured trumpet. I stayed at the Savoy until early in 1929. All of us boys got to be good friends and had learned to swing real hot together. But early in 1929, as I said, the Savoy got into some trouble or other and couldn't pay us. It was the end of the season in Chicago and there the band was without any engagement at all and most of the boys needing to make a living week by week. We talked over what we should do, and then we said, "Let's take a chance and bust cold into New York." Well, everybody liked the idea. Carroll was still the leader, of course, but he was not so well known then in New York, so he and the others said the band should be put in my name because I had been there and knew a few people, and Harlem had come to know a little about me, and maybe my name would help us get an engagement. We had not realized how much

they had been hearing about us, as we found out when
we reached New York.

We decided that each of us would take along just
twenty dollars. Four of us had little automobiles, so
we filled them up with gas and all piled in and started
for the big town, wondering what we would do when we
got there, but believing we would find something all
right. Anyhow, we were going to stick together. I only
took along twenty dollars, like the other boys, and left
the rest of my money with Lil to take care of the home
while I was away on this wild-goose chase. I had a kid
on my hands, too — I forgot to mention I had adopted
a son, a cousin of mine named Clarence Armstrong, and
was bringing him up. He's twenty-one years old now.

We got away from old Chicago, which had been mighty
good to me and given me my real start, and began stopping at all the big towns we passed. It was nice for us
to see the welcome we got everywhere — they had heard
us over the radio and we found we had quite a reputation. They wouldn't let us spend money for anything.
We would go to a cabaret and sit in with the local band
for a few numbers and eat and drink with them, and
there wouldn't be any check to pay. All the "cats" were
glad to see us. We took our time; we didn't have any
job to go to so we didn't care about hurrying and just
lazed along from one town to another, having real good
fun. We stopped in Detroit and Dayton and Cleveland
and other places, and when we got to Buffalo we decided
we would like to see Niagara Falls, so we drove on out

there. We didn't want to miss anything. Carroll's car never did reach New York—it got smashed up on the road and the boys in it had to double up in the other cars. My old bus made it, but was blowing off steam plenty when we rolled into Times Square.

The first thing I did when I reached New York was to call on Mr. Tommy Rockwell. He was the one who had arranged for me to make records in Chicago. He is now one of the partners of the firm of Rockwell-O'Keefe, in New York, and has a big and prosperous business, representing many famous stars, including Bing Crosby and many others. So I walked into Mr. Rockwell's office and said, "Well, I've got my band here." He said, "What do you mean, your band?" I said, "Well, I've got them anyway," and he said, "No use sending them back."

At that time, which was the top of the big boom years, there were three really big and famous night clubs in Harlem. They were "The Cotton Club," "Small's" and "Connie's Inn." They were the hottest late-at-night spots in New York and people who had money to spend and time to spend it in came from all over Manhattan to these clubs, even though they were five miles away from the theatre district. They would start up after theatres were out and get there around midnight. The clubs stayed open until morning. They all had very elaborate and wonderfully trained floor shows, featuring the most talented colored performers in the whole country who all flocked to Harlem in those days, even though they had to ride the rods to get there. Many of them became famous because of the chance they got to strut their stuff at those clubs. In the audience, any old night, would be famous actresses and critics and authors and publishers and rich Wall Street men and big people of all kinds, being gay and enjoying the hot swing music and the fast-stepping floor shows. Everybody, of course, was in evening clothes. They had to "dress" to get in. My, the money they spent in those days in those Harlem Clubs ! A gentleman and lady would have to spend from forty to sixty dollars for one evening, without spending money for wine. It was during prohibition and the clubs could not sell liquor, although the waiters and cap- tains often took a chance and cleaned up selling it under- cover at terrible prices — ten dollars for a pint and so on. So most of the people would bring their own drinks in flasks and buy bottled soda or ginger-ale at one dollar apiece for a little "splits" bottle, good for one tall drink. They would pay three dollars for an order of chicken- à-la-King or a seafood Newburgh, forty cents for a black coffee and so on — and all of that on top of a cover charge of perhaps seven to ten dollars. It was pretty bad, but they could afford it then and they had a good time. I guess a lot of them wished later they had held on to the money they spent in those days in the Harlem night clubs. But that's water gone over the dam. It isn't that way today. No, suh !

In less than a month after we boys landed in New York we had a big opportunity. It was now about Sep-

tember. This is how it happened. Leroy Smith had
had his band in Connie's Inn, on Lenox Avenue, Harlem (that was long before Connie's finally moved down
into the Broadway theatre district). Connie had organized and produced an all-colored musical revue, called
Hot Chocolates which was a hit and playing to big
houses at the Hudson Theatre on Broadway. He had
taken his cast from the Harlem night clubs, the cream
of the best colored performers. Connie wanted Leroy
Smith's orchestra for the show, so he pulled them out
of Connie's Inn and needed a good band to take their
place. And then we showed up. We got the job, and
were we lucky! Coming into the big town like that and
landing plump into one of the top spots in all New York,
all in a month. After we got our band in, I had another
big break for myself. Connie asked me to double with
Leroy Smith in the revue, playing feature trumpet numbers during the entr'act, and after the show, joining my
band at the Inn.

It was in *Hot Chocolates* that I introduced the song,
Ain't Misbehavin', playing a trumpet solo in the high
register. From the first time I heard it, that song used
to "send" me. I wood-shedded it until I could play all
around it. It was like *Heebie-Jeebies* and *Chinatown*
and *Treasure Island,* one of those songs you could cut
loose and swing with. When we opened, I was all ready
with it and it would bring down the house, believe me!
I believe that great song, and the chance I got to play it,
did a lot to make me better known all over the country.

I tell you, I have been lucky, and I have had a good manager, which I think is a good combination for anybody in show business to have. And I think they don't go very far as a rule without either one or the other.

X. CALIFORNIA, HERE I COME

"Hot Chocolates" had a long run for Broadway, where over two hundred plays and shows open every season and only a handful of them ever last as much as three months. In normal years there are about fifty legitimate theatres running in the Broadway district, all packed in one square mile, and all trying for a "hit." Over two hundred thousand people go to the theatre every week in New York, from the end of September to late in March. You don't find anything like that in any other place in the world. New Yorkers really love and understand the theatre and they are very quick to like a show or turn it down cold. Generally it is a "hit" the first week or it "flops." The producers know this, and that is why they will kill a show right away rather than risk any more loss on it, because it costs from ten thousand dollars up just to raise the curtain on an average, simple play, and perhaps a hundred thousand and up to open an elaborate musical show or revue before a dollar comes in. There is no chance-taking greater than show business for everybody concerned in it, from producer down to a "walk-on" actor.

Hot Chocolates, with a star cast and that grand song in it, ran through the winter and on into the spring of 1930 before it closed. When that happened, Leroy

Smith's band went back into Connie's Inn for the summer run, and Carroll Dickerson's band, with no "spot"
open, disbanded and some of the boys went back to Chicago. It's an old saying in the orchestra field, "Lose your
engagement and you lose your band." The boys have to
make a living somehow and can't just wait around, so
they naturally drift off into other jobs with other bands,
taking the best they can get, because they have to.

It was at this time that I first teamed up with Lew
Russell. Lew is one of our greatest swing pianists.
He is a very sensitive and very subtle musician who
hates tin-pan jazz as much as Mr. Jascha Heifitz or Mr.
Toscanini would. He had organized a twelve-piece band
of hand-picked swing players and was going out on a
long summer tour, mostly through the South. He heard
that I was free and offered to put his band in my name
and take me along as featured trumpeter.

That tour, which lasted six months, was the beginning
of a friendship and collaboration between Lew Russell
and me that has lasted to this day, for just this past winter
I had Lew's band in Connie's Inn, which is now down
on Broadway, and I am taking the boys on tour with me
this summer. I am sure this is one of the finest aggrega-
tions of colored swing players, all in one band, that you
will find in the world today, and this is largely due to
Lew Russell's wonderful musicianship and patience with
his men. When I am swinging trumpet out in front
of them, with my back to them, I always know that however far I swing away from the music we are playing,

wherever the trumpet carries them, they will be right in there following close, hot and sure of their rhythm, and never losing their way for one second — it's just as though they could see right through my back and know what's coming next almost as soon as I do. This is the band you hear over the radio when I play.

Later that year I made my first visit to Hollywood. I was booked at Sebastian's Cotton Club which is a famous Hollywood night club, and the band was put in my name. Hollywood certainly gave me a fine big hand. Every night the place would be full of movie stars and all of the hot musicians along the coast would come to hear us play. We broadcast every night, too, so California got a good load of us. With Sebastian's Cotton Club band, I made the following records, some of which may be remembered: *Memories of You, Ding Dong Daddy, Body and Soul, I'm Confessin', If I Could Be With You One Hour Tonight, You're Drivin' Me Crazy, Just a Gigolo, Shine, You're Lucky To Me,* and *I'm in the Market for You.*

I was in Hollywood almost a year that first trip, and then in 1931 I went on back to Chicago and began to get a band of my own together. I picked these boys: Charlie Alexander, piano, Preston Jackson, trombone, Mike McKendricks, banjo, Fred ("Tubby") Hall, drummer, George James, first alto sax, Lester Boone, second alto sax, "Al" Washington, tenor sax, Zilner T. Randolph, second trumpet, Johnny Lindsay, bass violin and myself, first trumpet. With this band I made recordings for OKEH records: *Them There Eyes, When Your Lover Has Gone, Little Joe, You Can Depend on Me.* Before that, for Victor, I had made: *High Society, Hustling and Bustling, Sitting in the Dark, I've Got a Right to Sing the Blues* and *I've Got the World on a String.*

For about six weeks, in the spring of 1931, I had this band in the Show Boat cabaret, on the Loop, and then I took them out on the longest road tour I had ever made to that time. It was some trip, believe me. We covered most all of the South and Southwest and must have played upwards of fifty or sixty cities, going out and coming in. And in between I had my first visit back to my old home in New Orleans since I had left nine years before.

We reached New Orleans early in June, and the last of the magnolias were still on the trees, the smell of them on the air. I did not know whether they had forgotten about me in all the time I'd been away, because I was just "Little Louie" Armstrong when I left and not too much account. But I soon found they had not. When our train pulled into the old L. & N. Station out by the Mississippi, at the head of Canal Street, I heard hot music playing. I looked out of the car window and could hardly believe what I saw. There, stretched out along the track, were eight bands, all swinging together, waiting to give us a big welcome. As soon as I got off the train the crowd went crazy. They picked me up and put me on their shoulders and started a parade down the center of Canal Street. Those eight bands almost bust the town open, they made so much noise. Everybody had a good time and I guess the police did too, because they didn't bother us at all. When they had marched around through the city they took me to my hotel for a little rest. My, it is a wonderful feeling to go back to your home town and find that while you have been away you have become a big man. I think that day was the happiest day in my life. All the New Orleans newspapers printed stories about how I had once been a newsboy and an inmate of the Waif's Home and how I had gone away and made good and now come back home. It was sure good. Yeah, man!

I had looked forward to seeing my old friends at home, and was sorry to find many of them had gone away, as I had, and were not there. Kid Ory wasn't there—he was in California. Zutti was still in Chicago. "Fate" Marable had left the *Dixie Belle* and was in St. Louis. "Papa Joe" Oliver, too, was up north. But I was mighty glad to see Davey Jones. He told me he was proud to have helped me get started and I told him I would always know what he had done to put me on my way in teaching me to read music on the *Dixie Belle*.

From June to August we played to packed houses at the Suburban Gardens and broadcast every night.

On the way north from New Orleans we played five weeks in St. Louis — a very fine run — and I met some more of my friends from the old river days. The long tour ended up in New York, in the Lafayette Theatre in Harlem. Then I went to Hollywood again, playing with

Les Hites at the Cotton Club there. After three or four months I decided I needed a good rest and vacation and that I would like to see Europe. So I bought myself an old Buick and drove it east to Chicago. After seeing Lil and attending to some things there, I took a train to New York, said goodbye to my friends in Harlem and sailed on the *Majestic,* of the White Star Line, for England. On that trip I was to get a new idea about swing music.

XI. *HIGHSEAS AND HIGH C's*

THE first day I was in London, the musicians and critics
gave me a reception at the Ambassador. I almost
missed it because my trunks hadn't come and I didn't
have anything to put on. They got there just in time
and I went down and everybody was mighty nice to me
and made me feel right away I was with friends. Some
of the big critics from the London newspapers were there
and asked me all kinds of questions about how swing was
doing in America. I told them it was doing fine. One
thing sure did surprise me. A lot of the musicians asked
me if it wasn't true that when I hit my high-C's on the
records I had a clarinet take the notes. They had not
thought it really was my trumpet getting up there on C.
Some of them wanted to look at my trumpet, thinking I
had invented some kind of gadget for it so I could play
high register. And they weren't satisfied until they
handed me a trumpet they had with them and had me
swing it. Then they cheered and everybody had to have
a good laugh on them and of course they laughed too.

I didn't have any band to play with and was booked to
open at the Palladium Theatre which is one of the big
vaudeville theatres. We wired to Paris to rush some
good swing musicians over to London. They got there
in time. I was mighty glad to see Peter du Congé from

New Orleans among them! We had a nice talk about home. Also my friend Charley Johnson was along. There were several colored French musicians and I had to talk to them through an interpreter, but, as I have said before, all swing men can talk together and understand each other through their music, so we got along fine.

Well, we broke the all-time record at the Palladium for a band! We were at the top of the bill and out in big lights. We played at the Palladium for two weeks to standing room only. At the end of our engagement, one of the very nicest things that was ever done for me happened. The management of the Palladium appreciated very much the big success we had had and the big crowds of people and the newspaper notices which we had brought to the theatre. To show me how pleased they were, they presented me with a beautiful gold French Selmer trumpet with my name engraved on it. This is the trumpet you see in the picture at the front of this book and it is the one I like best to play because I think Selmer trumpets have the purest, finest tone of any trumpets I know about. I still use this trumpet today and probably will until it's worn out, which will be a good long time. After the record engagement at the Palladium the boys in the band had to get back to Paris, so I got together a ten-piece band of white swing-men and for the next four months we toured all over England and Scotland and were welcomed by big crowds everywhere. It was a fine tour, believe me. In that band were Lou Davis, Billie Mason, Allan Ferguson, Buddie Featherstonehaugh, Len Berman, Bruts Gonella and others about as good.

When I went back to New Orleans and got that big welcome I was surprised. But I could figure out it was because I was a home-town boy and everybody wanted to be nice to me. When I landed in England and found the welcome I got everywhere I was a whole lot more surprised and at first I just couldn't figure it out at all. I didn't see how all of these people over there could have come to hear about me, let alone want to make so much fuss over me. Pretty soon I began to understand. They were record fans. There are hundreds of thousands of these record fans all over Europe. They buy new records as fast as they're made, the way Americans buy the latest popular magazines and the way Americans used to buy records before the radio came. That is because, in Europe, the radio stations do not carry nearly so much modern music, but more classical programs, so the people who like the newer music get it on records. And mostly from American recordings. There was the answer. People all around Europe had been hearing me on records, Gennett, Victor, OKEH, Brunswick, Decca, for eight years past, until I guess they had come to feel they sort of knew me, or at least wanted to see what I was like. Each record had been a piece of bread cast on the waters for me, but I hadn't ever realized it before. My record of *You Rascal, You* had gone over especially big in England.

Then there was another thing which was important and that was the rhythm or "hot" clubs. Europe, you remember, had gone pretty crazy over American jazz towards the end of the war when the Dixieland first arrived in London in 1917. Then came Jim Europe and other early American jazz bands and later, Duke Ellington, Cab Calloway and other famous jazz combinations of more recent years. From the first the European music critics, as I have said, took all of this new American music a lot more seriously than we did at home and wrote a great deal about it—we just liked it without thinking so much about it. And it is right to say they heard the very best of our bands and of our recordings and didn't have to listen to so much of the tin-panny kind of trash music that has made a lot of our home folks sick of any kind of jazz music—and I don't blame them much either.

XII. *RECORD FANS AND HOT CLUBS*

PRETTY soon the record fans and other followers of swing music began to form clubs and to publish their own music journals. These clubs are established now in every country in Europe and all keep in very close touch with one another. When counted all together they have hundreds of thousands of members. In England and Scotland there are almost fifty clubs, all joined in the British Rhythm Club Federation. The Federation publishes its own monthly music magazine called "Swing Music." The United Hot Clubs of France publishes its own magazine, called "Hot Jazz." They are all swing lovers, but in France they use the term "hot jazz" to mean the new music. The swing federations in the different countries now all work together through the International Federation of Hot Clubs. M. Hugues Panassié, who is president of the Hot Club of Paris and a leading French Music critic, is President of the International Federation and Mr. M. W. Stearns, a well-known American swing critic, is secretary. I may mention that M. Panassié has published a very interesting book on swing music, called, "Le Jazz Hot," and that another French critic, M. Robert Goffin, also has published a book called, "On the Frontiers of Jazz." I was very surprised and pleased when I found that this second book was dedicated "To Louis Armstrong, the Real King of Jazz, in testimony of my high admiration." Both of these books are carefully written and will be very interesting to anyone who wants to study modern music. The members of these European clubs include thousands of amateur musicians and many of the finest musical technicians and critics abroad. They have followed jazz for a long time and watched it slowly grow away from its cruder melodies and its set syncopations and become real swing music. And too, they have done a lot over there to develop swing music — much more than Americans know. They believe it is an important advance in the history of all music and are working together to have it recognized that way. I am sure they will succeed. Perhaps a hundred years from now, people will remember these clubs for their work.

Now I know there are a lot of people who will read this book who will say that "swing" is just a new name for the same old jazz they've been hearing for many years and that I am trying to make it look as though it was something new. Even some of the editors of the publishing house which is publishing this book told me that at first, though of course in a very polite way. But I cannot say too strongly to these people that there is all the difference in the world and if they will just try to understand it they will very soon be singing out when they tune in a band on their radios, "That's swing!" or "That's not swing," and will be able to tell at once.

Now the *basic idea* of swing music is not new. The

swing idea of free improvisation by the players was at the core of jazz when it started back there in New Orleans thirty years ago.   Those early boys were swing-men, though they didn't know so much about it then as we do today.   But they had the *basic idea,* all right. What happened was that this idea got lost when jazz swept over the country.   I think the reason it got over-looked and lost was that when the public went crazy over jazz the music publishing companies and the record companies jumped in and had all the songs written down and recorded and they and the theatre producers and northern dance halls paid our boys more money than they'd ever heard of to help write down and play these songs.   Popular songs before jazz had always been played the way they were written and that was what made "song hits" for the publishers.   So the commercial men wanted the new jazz tunes played the same way so the public would come to learn them easily and sing them.   The public liked that, too, because the new tunes were "catchy" and different and people liked to sing them and hear them played that way.   Jazz was new to them and they didn't understand it enough to be ready for any "crazy business."   So most of the good jazz players and jazz bands which followed the Dixieland Five went down the easiest road where the big money was, and you can hardly blame them when you look back now and see how few people understood what it was really all about anyway.   Some of the boys stuck along and just wouldn't follow scoring, it wasn't in 'em, and some of the others that didn't learn to read music went on swinging the way they had learned to love. Very few of them ever made much money, but playing in small clubs and dives they kept swing alive for many years. Then there was another group of the boys who took a straddle and I think they were the smartest and that they have probably done more to bring swing into its own than anybody. They were the swing-men who went on into the commercial field, joined big conventional bands, played the game as it was dished out to them and made their money, and yet who loved swing so much that they kept it up outside of their regular jobs. They did it through the jam sessions held late at night after their work was done. It makes me think of the way the early Christians would hold their meetings in the catacombs under Rome. With those musicians I guess it was the old saying: "He who fights and runs away will live to fight another day." At any rate, the truth is that most of the best-known swing artists of today are or were the crack-shot musicians with big conventional bands (name bands, we call them because they are usually known by the name of their leader) or on big radio programs, but they don't miss their jam sessions where they can cut loose as they please, with or without a leader, feel their own music running through them and really enjoy themselves. These swing-men who have come up to the top because of their musicianship are slowly having an influence on the big bands they play with. Some of them have become so popular with the public that they now have their own bands and can do more what they like to do, like Mr. "Red" Norvo, Mr. Benny Goodman, Mr. Tommy Dorsey, Mr. Jimmy Dorsey, Mr. "Red" Nichols, Mr. Earl Hines, Mr. Chick Webb, Mr. "Fats" Waller, Mr. Teddy Hill and others.

My publishers suggested to me that it would be interesting to some of my readers if I should give a list of the great swing musicians of today, the men who are making swing history, and I have thought a lot about it because I would like to do any little thing I could to help the public know more about some of the swing-men who are not in the "big-time" but who are tops among musicians. But the more I have thought about it, the more I am afraid to try — because there are hundreds of good men — both at home and in Europe — and sure as could be I would leave out somebody who ought to be in and I would not want to do that. So I have just talked in this book about the men whom I happened to know best in my own career. But before I do close this story of swing music, I can and must pay tribute to two men now dead who were among our pioneers and whose memory is honored by every swing man who ever heard them play — "Bix" Beiderbecke, hot trumpet, and Eddie Lang, hot guitarist. They both rose to fame in Mr. Paul Whiteman's early Chicago Band, the band that also featured such great swing players as Mr. Jack Teagarden, trombone, Mr. Frank Trumbauer, sax, Mr. Jimmy Dorsey, clarinet, and Mr. Lennie Hayton, piano.

The European hot clubs have been going on for years but only in 1935 did the idea spread back to the homeland of swing.   In October, 1935, the United Hot Clubs of America was launched.   Mr. John Hammond, a prominent music writer and critic, was made president and Mr. M. W. Stearns, secretary.   The American Federation announced it was "dedicated to the universal progress of swing music."   It started with these seven clubs : New York Hot Club, Milton Gabler, president, Warren W. Scholl, secretary, Yale Hot Club (New Haven), M. W. Stearns, president, Chicago Hot Club, Helen Oakley, president; Squirrel Ashcraft, treasurer, Jack Howe, secretary, Cleveland Hot Club, William H. Cloverdale, president, Lee White, Jr., secretary, Boston Hot Club, George Frazier, president, Los Angeles Hot Club, Chauncey P. Farrer, president.   I think all American swing lovers should support these new American hot clubs, the way Europeans have supported their clubs, and that new clubs should be formed in other cities and colleges.   It only costs two dollars a year to be a member, and any musician will get back many times that amount in what he will learn and the fun he will have meeting other swing-men and "jamming" with them.   And, as the Federation's new monthly bulletin says : "Swing music is one of the unique American contributions to the world.   The fact that, like our poets Walt Whitman and Edgar Allen Poe, it was first truly appreciated abroad, adds to our obligation to study it and spread an understanding of it at home.   Like the skyscraper, it remains typically American." I think that is true, and I have seen myself what Europe thinks of our home-brand swing. And that takes me along back to my own story.

When we got back to London, I went over to have a look at Paris and take a little rest for a week before I had to get back home. I landed in New York the day President Roosevelt was elected, November 2, 1932. It had been a short trip but I got home thinking swing music was a lot more important than I knew before, and I guess maybe I was feeling a little important about my own playing, too — you know how you can get sometimes. Those high-C's certainly did wow 'em. Man!

XIII. *SWINGING THROUGH EUROPE*

DURING the next six months I toured over the United States again with my own bands. Then, in July of 1933, I sailed again from New York for Europe. I decided on this trip I would try to see more of the Continent and learn all I could from the European swingmen.

I got a nice welcome back to England when I opened at the Holbern Empire Theatre. My manager had to go back home, so soon after I got to London I started to get my own band together. I brought some of our best men over from Paris again, and acted as manager of the band and conductor too. I wood-shedded with the boys day and night until we began to work up real hot together. I wanted that band to be good and no mistake. I planned to keep them with me for at least a year and take them on a long tour. I know that being billed as an American swing band wherever we went the people would look at us for something extra special in the way of hot music and I wanted to give 'em a load of how we swing that music at home. My "cats" understood it the same way and began lickin' their chops, as we say it. Pretty soon we were ready to "go to town" together any old time we would play. It was good.

We played England that summer of 1933 and in the

fall. The members of the Rhythm clubs were very kind
to us everywhere we went. One young man made me a
present which I will always treasure. It was a medieval
trumpet which had been in his family for many cen-
turies, back to the Middle Ages. It sure was a funny
old instrument, not as fine of course as our modern trumpets. When I blew it, I would think of how it probably
used to sing out in the courtyard of some old castle and
wondered about the trumpeter who used it and if he
would like to swing it. While I was in England I heard
that Miss Josephine Baker was there and was ill. I went
up and had a nice visit with her. I think she is a great
artist and wish she would spend more of her time at
home.

When the winter season of 1933-1934 came along we
were ready for our Continental tour. Our first big
engagement was at Copenhagen, Denmark. I guess
that was the biggest welcome, in number of people, I
ever got anywhere. The Copenhagen newspapers said
that ten thousand people greeted us at the station. All I
remember is a whole ocean of people all breaking through
the police lines and bearing down on us until I got afraid
we were going to get stomped underfoot. They pushed
a big trumpet, all made out of flowers, into my hands
and put me into an open automobile and started a
parade. The next day the newspapers carried my picture and big write-ups about our coming to Denmark.
You'd have thought I had been some kind of a national
hero to them. I suppose it was the record fans and

the Danish hot clubs.   At any rate I know I will never forget how kind those Copenhagen people were to Louis Armstrong and his band.   After that wonderful welcome, we gave eight concerts at the big concert hall in Lyric Park, every performance sold out and jammed. The proprietors told me they made twenty thousand dollars in those three days !   It shows what Europeans think of American swing music.   It's something to think about.

From Denmark, we crossed over to Stockholm, Sweden, and there another big crowd met us at the station and it was about the same thing all over again.   In Stockholm I was very pleased to have dinner one night with Marion Anderson, our fine colored concert singer, who was there at that time.   From Sweden, we went to Oslo, the capital of Norway and played there in the biggest concert hall in town to standing room.   We played a few other engagements in Norway, then crossed over Germany into Holland.   We played a fine engagement at the Ritz-Carlton in Amsterdam and then crossed back over the English Channel to London for our last run of that year.   It was at that time that we were honored by giving a performance before the then Prince of Wales and Prince George.   We sure "went to town" for the princes and I hope they liked it.

We had had a very hard year and I wanted to rest, so we broke up and I went to Paris and got an apartment where I could be quiet for a little.   I didn't want to do any more work just then, so I just lazed around for three or four months, meeting the swing musicians and critics and taking it easy. I did give two concerts at the Salle Playal. Cab Calloway and Duke Ellington had played there before me. A lot of the Americans in Paris came to hear me swing, and that pleased me very much. The French manager told me I had to go out and sing in French. I told him I wasn't going to sing any other way than I knew how to sing. He was pretty mad and said I would be a "flop." Anyway I got such a big hand I had to come out of my dressing room in my bathrobe for the curtain calls. I would have been a flop all right, trying to stand up there singing in French which I didn't know anything about. It would be like wanting Miss Lucienne Boyer to sing in English.

Just as I was about getting homesick again, and ready to take my boat, a European impresario, named N. J. Canneti, asked me if I would tour the Continent and I decided I might as well since he had most everything arranged. We played Belgium, including Brussels, Antwerp, Liége and other cities, and then toured down through France and into Italy. At Turino we played before the Crown Princess of Italy. I remember we spent New Year's Eve, 1935, in Lausanne, Switzerland. We went over the Alps into Switzerland by bus and that was a very thrilling thing to me. We saw Italian soldiers way up on the mountain sides moving along on skis. They went very fast.

When that trip ended up at Paris, I packed up and took my boat back to America. It seemed I had been gone ten years when we landed at New York, and was I glad to be back home!

From January of 1935 to May I took myself a good rest in Chicago. I saw Peter and Rags, which are my dogs. Then, with a fourteen-piece band, I started out down through the Middle West and into the South. We had an even bigger welcome than before. People were beginning now to understand more clearly the difference between a swing orchestra and an ordinary popular orchestra and were going strong for swing. By August we reached New Orleans again and they met me with another nice parade. After three days at home, we struck right north again and in the last week of August opened the fall season of the Howard Theatre in Washington and then went on to the Apollo Theatre in New York. At the Apollo we broke all records and received the highest salary ever paid a colored orchestra for a week's engagement. Shortly after that the band disbanded and went back to Chicago. In the first week of October, I opened at Connie's Inn on Broadway with Luis Russell's band behind me. My manager, Mr. Joe Glaser, had decided we would take over the management of this fine band, which I have spoken of before. During our long engagement at Connie's Inn, I broadcast again for the Columbia Broadcasting System over its coast-to-coast network.

Photograph by Richard Merrill

LOUIS ARMSTRONG AND HIS ORCHESTRA, BOSTON, 1936

XIV. *JAM !*

WHEN we grew up in New Orleans we learned to swing without books. There weren't any books written about that kind of music — it was all too new yet — and if there had been books they wouldn't have done us much good because most of us hadn't learned to read music, as I have said. Later on, when we did learn, we travelled a lot faster.

And even now, thirty years after Swing was born, this book is the first history of swing music, and of the men who made it, to be published in the English language.

Today most of the young musicians understand the value of knowing how to read music and many amateur musicians are expert readers at an early age. I know because I have talked with thousands of young swing-men, all over the country. They are able to get some good out of a book, so I especially want to make this first book on swing truly helpful to students and amateurs and young musicians everywhere. I hope the first part of this book, up to here, will give them, as well as non-musicians and general readers, some idea of the long struggle swing music had to go through to arrive where it has arrived today and of the kind of men who brought it through. The second part of the book, entitled, "Music Section," I have planned exclusively for the use of young musicians and students of swing music. In preparing this section, I have had the generous co-opera-tion of some of the world's greatest living swing players. You will know them by their names. I also have had the valuable assistance of Mr. Horace Gerlach, a keen student of swing music who has made many special arrangements for my bands. He has edited the Music Section and assisted in arranging the illustrative scores. The illustrations will show the young musician on any of the ten important swing instruments, how one of the great masters of that instrument swings a given selection. I do not suggest that the reader *copy* anyone else in play-ing his own instrument, in fact, I want to warn him not to because his own originality is very important if he, too, is to become a master swingman. But I am sure at the same time that a careful study of the illustrations will open up some doors of musical understanding of swing as it is now played by our most advanced musi-cians. I am, of course, most fond of the trumpet, and for the benefit of all young trumpeters I have myself con-tributed an illustration of how I swing with this instru-ment. The Music Section also includes a new and unpublished swing song, composed for this book by Mr. Gerlach and myself and named "Swing That Music." I believe it will become really popular, for it is "good swing."

Another very helpful thing for amateurs, as I have said, is to play frequently with other swingmen in jam sessions — in fact this practice and the exchanging of new

ideas is, I think, very important. One or two jam sessions, with some good, free players, will sometimes teach
a man more than playing six months with a regular band.
For musicians living in or near New York City there are
at least five places where they can go and jam almost
any night of the winter season, around midnight. They
are The Onyx Club and The Famous Door on West 52nd
Street between Fifth and Sixth Avenues, The Hickory
House, on West 52nd Street, one block farther west,
Adrian's Tap Room in The President Hotel on West
48th Street, and, in Harlem, the Rhythm Club, at 132nd
Street and Seventh Avenue.

XV. *I HOPE GABRIEL LIKES OUR MUSIC*

SWING musicians have to work hard and they have had difficulties in their way that "regular" musicians have not had. This was more true in the early days than it is today, and with the many good young swingmen now coming up in the ranks and the growing popular understanding of swing music the situation is changing around very fast. Swing has been coming on especially strong in the last two or three years. I think the sensational success of swing bands on the radio has had a good deal to do with it.

So I would say that the future for real swing musicians is very bright indeed, especially for the younger men. If I should be asked to advise one of these young men what to do to become a front-rank swing player, I would urge him to learn to read expertly and be just as *able* to play to score as any "regular" musician. Then I would tell him never to forget for one minute of his life that the true spirit of swing music lies in free playing and that he must always keep his own musical feeling free. He must try always to originate and not just imitate. And if he is a well-trained musician in the first place, he will be able to express his own musical ideas, as they come to him, with more versatility, more richness and more "body" than if he is poorly trained. To be a real swing artist, he must be a composer as well as a player.   A young man who is just willing to follow his score, and stop there, can never be a swingman, no matter how many swing songs he plays on his fiddle. And I say to young men, paste that sentence on your instrument rack !

Yes, swing musicians worked hard for a quarter of a century, and against odds, to bring swing to the top and the swing musicians of this day have their work cut out for them to carry their art forward, to develop swing music into a broad and rich American music.   That means plenty of work for everybody and plenty of room, too, for anybody with true musical feeling who wants to help.

The way I look at swing music as it stands today is that it is America's second big bid to bring forth a worthwhile music of its own.   The first big attempt was in the early days of jazz.   We can look back now and see the mistakes and see about where jazz got side-tracked. We won't have many excuses to make if we let today's swing music go the same way.   Jazz lost its originality and freshness and stopped growing.   It stopped early.   As it came to be written down and recorded in all the thousand and one jazz songs of later years, it was not musically rich enough.   Take almost any one of those songs, even the big hits, and keep playing it over the way it was composed and written and pretty soon it gets tiresome and you want to hear a new tune.   That is why you got a big vogue for one tune and then in a few months it sounded stale and a vogue for another one would come along. And yet many of those songs had a lot to them underneath, as I know.   My own swing orchestra can take one of the old favorites, like *Chinatown* and swing it so that a new kind of beauty and a fuller "body" comes into it.   Another old-timer we swing is the great pioneer jazz song, *St. Louis Blues*.   That was written back in 1914 and it still stands head and shoulders above most. Jazz needed constant improvisation and experimentation before it could grow into a richer music.

The writers of jazz have not developed jazz music much during all these years, although a few men must be given credit.   But for the most part the new songs that have been coming out of "Tin Pan Alley," which is Broadway's music publishing district, are not really new at all.   They are the same old melodies and rhythms just twisted around in a different way and with different words.   Coarse beats or sticky-sweet phrases and all that, year after year.   It makes a good musician tired and it is no wonder to me at all that a big part of the public is tired of it, too.   And, of all the people who like it least are the swing musicians, for they are the very ones who are doing most to break up these worn-out patterns. The reason swing musicians insist upon calling their music "swing music" is because they know how different it is from the stale brand of jazz they've got so sick of hearing.   But in the early days when jazz was born, jazz wasn't that way at all — it was the first crude form of today's swing, the daddy of swing and it was "going places" until it got all tangled up in "Tin Pan Alley" and made fortunes for men who couldn't swing a jew's-harp.   And that is the real truth at the bottom of it all.

I am glad that I am only thirty-six years old now. Jazz and I got born together and grew up side by side when we were poor.   I knew jazz before it began to go soft with too much success coming too early.   I saw it try to put on spats before it got used to walking in shoes, and I think that is not too good for any young man or any young art.   I saw it start travelling in flashy company and pretty much go bad for a good many years. Just a few of us old friends remembered the good kid we used to know in the honky tonks of New Orleans, on the Mississippi river boats and in the dance halls on Chicago's old South Side.

Today, when I am thirty-six, swing music has arrived. I think I will live to see it come into a very great future. I am sure the idea of it and the spirit of it are right and that it is an art in the true sense.   I want to see our young swingmen keep it that way.   And I say to them, and to all of my friends and all swing lovers,

"I Hope Gabriel Likes Our Music."

PART TWO

MUSIC SECTION

Edited by
HORACE GERLACH

I. INTRODUCTION TO SWING

Louis Armstrong's story of the evolution of modern American music has traced its growth from the barbaric phase through to today's refined and developed forms. As he has shown, the rigid and pronounced beat of the tom-tom and the startling and exciting melodies of the tribal and revival chants and songs have become softened and tempered, and vastly enriched, by the influences of classical music. We have achieved a form of rhythmic and melodic expression that is graceful. Our music discloses elements of the polka and the schottische, the grace of the waltz and the delicacy of the minuet. Instead of a definite and coarsely accentuated beat, we have a more elastic tempo. In place of gruff, shrill, awkward and unpolished melody, we hear new strains that are sympathetic, more closely integrated, of higher musical quality and character and flowing with more evenness and suavity.

Louis Armstrong has been in the vanguard of those who have brought about this vast progress in the short span of three decades. Through ceaseless improvisation and experimentation, Armstrong and that comparatively limited group of brilliantly gifted men who have shared with him great natural talent and musical integrity are forging a new American music.   Besides Armstrong himself, nine of the foremost figures in this elect group of swing musicians kindly have contributed to this Music Section.

Apart from the important rôle that he has played as a pioneer experimenter, Armstrong, by common agreement, is the greatest living virtuoso on his own instrument, the trumpet.   His improvised trumpet solos have become classics in the literature of swing music.   His solo work displays two aspects, one purely melodic and the other more dependent upon rhythmic melody.   The melodic aspect is strongly emphasized by his use of arpeggios, chords whose principal tones are segregated.   By skipping up or down in natural sequence, from one note to the next in position, he produces concordant melody. His demonstrations with chords on the trumpet are unique.   His progression from one chord to another reveals him as a master of modulation.   Any group of notes that he plays in a chord stands forth as an independent melody.   The ensuing phrases flow in perfect continuity — as evenly as a poet's verse.   His rhythmic expressions illustrate superlative command of both simple and involved syncopation.

II. ARMSTRONG IN THE UPPER REGISTER

Armstrong is celebrated, of course, for his amazing fluency in the higher register of his instrument.   This is partly explained by his great physical endurance. There is a great deal of resistance in playing high notes on the trumpet because the lips are severely contracted and little air can pass through them.   In order to force air through the small opening in the lips, the abdominal muscles must exert great pressure.   The more tightly the lips are pressed together the more they vibrate when air is forced between them.   Each increase in the rate of vibration produces a higher note.   Through years of ceaseless effort, Armstrong has hardened his lip and jaw muscles and developed his abdominal air pressure to the point where he can strike and hold a high C for a greater length of time than any living swing trumpeter.   When in this register, it is a battle between stomach muscles and face muscles; out of a great issuing power, held firmly in restraint at the point of issuance, comes the incredible beauty of his high notes, notes golden in purity, never wavering, never shrill.   An example of his control of the high register may be found in his rendition for records of *When You're Smiling,* which he plays an octave higher than written.   A majority of the notes in the last chorus are on or above high C, which he holds with comparative ease.   Frequently he plays up to high F and G, three and four tones, respectively, above C.

III.   RHYTHMIC COUNTERPOINT

Armstrong makes good use of his high note dexterity to aid him in achieving his rhythmical counterpoint.

He strikes piercing notes with the regularity of a trip
hammer and emits long and short "screams" from his
trumpet bell.   This style of counterpoint is perhaps best
illustrated in his recordings of *Chinatown* and *Swing
That Music.* The *Chinatown* recording shows the man-
ner in which Armstrong employs his high note technique
to produce an effective rhythmic counterpoint.   Just
as the cinder-path runner adjusts and develops his pace,
so Armstrong develops his progression in *Chinatown*.
He warms up slowly, swinging along at an even stride.
At the second chorus he speeds up his phrases a bit and
uses more effort.   The third chorus finds him stretching
out and covering more territory, spreading out his musical passages to cover a wider range.   In the fourth chorus
we hear him as we see the runner in the heat.   The
speed and motion are regulated at a metered rhythm.
This continues until the last lap, or chorus, when the
sprint is necessary.   Then at the last strain we seem to
see the runner sprint for those few remaining yards as
we hear Armstrong's trumpet mount higher and his notes
come faster and more forcefully.   The last lunge is felt
as Armstrong reaches for that highest of notes which he
strikes like the racer breaking the tape at the finish.
The leisurely start, the stretching out, the building up,
the sprint, the spurt and the climax.   There are many
solos by Armstrong on the style of *Chinatown* and *Swing
That Music,* including *St. Louis Blues, Dinah, You Rascal, You, Tiger Rag* and others worthy of examination.
When playing these songs he uses more of a staccato

rhythmic melody than in the ballads or slow swing songs where he mostly employs a flowing melody very much in the nature of an obbligato. In some instances he plays one note for thirty-two bars, striking each tone at regular intervals. One of his novelties is to play a hundred consecutive high C's (his world record is 280!) and then elaborate on this remarkable feat by ending with F above high C. You will notice in his recording of *Chinatown* the absence of smoothly connected melody line, it being supplanted by single tones of half-note value or more, depicting a rhythmic nature rather than a purely melodic one. It gives the listeners a feeling of locomotion and is very exciting as it races along.

IV. SWING INTERPOLATION

It is likewise notable that when playing a fast selection Armstrong usually avoids using groups of notes in rapid progression. These quickly executed passages are unnoticed or lost in the fury of a careening tempo. By sustaining tones against the rapid motions of the rhythmic background (drums, piano, bass, guitar) he perfects a contrast that enables his reproduction to stand out, as a stable object would in front of shifting scenery. This is somewhat similar to playing a melody of a song halftime while the accompaniment proceeds in the designated tempo. This is the only time Armstrong plays definite melodic progression in fast numbers. A great trick of his is to interpolate other melodies foreign to the song being played. He may interpolate any melody that fits the chording of the composition being treated. He sometimes uses operatic strains in *Dinah* or *Tiger Rag* and they cohere flawlessly. Some of the songs used this way are *Gipsy Sweetheart, Rigoletto, Swanee River, Johnny, Get Your Gun, Rustle of Spring, Exactly Like You, National Emblem, Lady Be Good, Confessin', The Song is Ended,* and the strain *Going Home* from a famous symphony by Dvorák.

Examples of Armstrong's interpolations include:

1. The first strain of *Exactly Like You* to the background of *Dinah.*
2. The first sixteen bars of *National Emblem* combined with *Tiger Rag.*
3. The first eight bars of *Confessin'* interpolated in *Tiger Rag.*
4. The first few bars of *The Song Is Ended, Going Home,* and *Swanee River* used with *St. Louis Blues.*
5. The first few strains of *Johnny, Get Your Gun* used in *Chinatown.*
6. *Lady Be Good* and *Gipsy Sweetheart* used with *Dinah.*

In his interpolations the interpolated melodies employed, such as Dvorák's *New World Symphony* strains, *Exactly Like You,* and *Johnny, Get Your Gun,* are slow-moving in contrast to the rapid tempos of *St. Louis Blues* (He plays this song unusually fast), *Chinatown,* and *Dinah.* There are exceptions when he plays a group of notes in rapid succession during numbers that have a fast tempo, such as the break in *Dinah* where he uses the strain from *Rigoletto*. When this is done, however, the band is tacit and his passage stands out unencumbered by the background of the orchestra.

The preceding discussion covers Armstrong's improvisation and execution of the fast moving, rhythmic type of trumpet solo. We may next consider another aspect of his solo work. This I have mentioned as having a purely melodic structure. He excels all swing exponents in the art of obbligato.

V. MELODIC COUNTERPOINT

Armstrong's version of *I Can't Give You Anything But Love* is one of his oldest and most beautiful recordings. In the last chorus he plays what is considered by many his most sonorous counter-melody. The saxophones carry the tune in the lower register and Armstrong counterpoints with his trumpet. The phrasing he uses and the choice selection of chord tones show the depth of his musical understanding. Listeners hardly notice the original song being played and pay most attention to this new melody he has created. His obbligatos should be of great value to arrangers of music. One can imagine a group of violins in a large orchestra playing in unison this type of obbligato as a counterpoint to some pastoral composition.

Armstrong can improvise melodies over a long period without repetition and with a great variety of rhythm and tonal sequences. In his progress from the Delta to the metropolis he had little contact with the classics. These he keenly appreciates. He has felt the influence of the masterpieces of composition though not fundamentally schooled in the *études* and the symphonies. If an occasion demanded his rendition on trumpet of the lovely song, *My Heart at Thy Sweet Voice* from *Sampson* and *Delilah,* or *Vesta Lagubla* from *Pagliacci,* he could with very little application accomplish this artistically and with brilliance. He is a true artist and a great stylist.

The rhythmic obbligato he inherits directly from his race. In his melodic obbligatos, the melody does not clash with that of the original song. He weaves in and out choosing the important chord tones and threading them into beautiful, independent strains. His counterpoint seems to be conversing with the song as it flows along in operatic-duet form. In order properly to interpret these musical illustrations, the student should have heard either Armstrong's recordings or some of his recitals. Then the musical ideas he has invented come to life. To those not acquainted with his work, I suggest procuring any of his available recordings or listening to his scheduled broadcasts.

In the recording of *I Can't Give You Anything But Love* observe closely Armstrong's melodic counterpoint! After you have studied it as an auxiliary interpolation, close your ears to the melody and concentrate on his obbligato. You will notice its richness, freshness, and independent structure. The counterpoint no longer needs the support of the song but stands alone as a new composition. It is very likely that a number of the popular songs of today were inspired by some phrase or idea occurring in Armstrong's contrapointal inventions.

VI. RHYTHMIC OBBLIGATO

Armstrong's rhythmic obbligato is not an abrupt syncopation. Each phrase seems to lean and fall forward and, before it lapses into a resting position, to be lifted up and carried forward again. His solos are unquestionably melodies counterpointed against the original songs. Separating the so-called obbligato from the song we find no trace of similarity between the two. His improvisations may be tinted and edged by the song used in each case, but the definite original melody is lacking. Notice how cleverly he segregates the chords to furnish melodic material. By combining chord tones, passing tones, and rhythms he has developed the melodic counterpoint and the ensuing rhythmic obbligatos. *Ain't Misbehavin'*, *Confessin'*, and *Lazy River* are striking examples.

VII. MELODIC OBBLIGATO

Another form of solo Armstrong plays is that in which he uses mostly the original song with slight syncopations occasionally digressing to a counterpoint. This is illustrated in his recordings of *Treasure Island, Falling in Love,* and *I'm in the Mood for Love.*

This style of playing is a very popular form of swing music because it preserves much of the original melody and thereby relieves the confusion of the listener who is not familiar with complicated swing improvisation. Swing musicians in the very freedom of their musical expression often leave out the melody to such an extent that the audience fails to recognize the basic song. Tunes presented with elaborate variations soon lose their identity. After one or two choruses, the swing performer, seeking to avoid repetition of a simple and tiring song melody, which he has tried to make interesting by the use of syncopation, delayed resolutions, additional cadences, and all kinds of embellishments, will then discard the boring and exhausted original melody and plunge into the chords for material to sustain him as he swings through the remaining choruses.

VIII.   EXAMPLES OF SWING ON TEN INSTRUMENTS

On the following pages is presented an original piano score especially written for this volume by Mr. Armstrong and myself.   It carries the title of the book, *Swing That Music*.

Ten of the foremost swing musicians have generously supplied original improvisations for their particular instruments to accompany the piano part.   Their brilliant interpretations appear on the succeeding pages.   Thus, an outstanding master of each of the instruments has shown how he might render *Swing That Music*.

GLOSSARY OF SWING TERMS

GUTBUCKET: Swing in Blues fashion, disconsolate.

IN THE GROOVE: When carried away or inspired by the music, when playing in exalted spirit and to perfection.

JAM SESSION: An informal meeting of musicians playing for their amusement, swinging without leadership or score, experimental session.

PAPERMAN: A musician who plays only written music, as written.

RIDE: Easy-going rhythm.

SCREW-BALL: Crazy, extremely unbridled swing.

WHACKY: Same as above, only noisier, more discordant.

OUT OF THE WORLD: Same as IN THE GROOVE.

WAXING: Recording for phonograph records.

ALLIGATOR: A non-playing swing devotee, a listener.

BARREL-HOUSE: Every man for himself, playing without regard for what the others are playing.

CATS: The musicians of a swing orchestra.

LICKING THEIR CHOPS: Getting warmed up to swing.

FRISKING THEIR WHISKERS: Same as above.

COFFEE-AND-CAKE: Very poor pay for a job, often only carfare.

COLLEGIATE: Extremely slow style swing music.

COMMERCIAL: Appealing to the uninitiated public, compromise swing.

CORNEY: The "razz-mah-jazz" style of the Twenties.

GANG: A medley of songs.

GETTING OFF: Commencing to swing.

LICK : An original interpolated phrasing.

BREAK : Dropping the rhythm for a few beats.

DIXIELAND : The original, New Orleans jazz as developed by the famous "Dixieland Five."

SOCK CHORUS : Last chorus of an arrangement.

MUGGING LIGHT : Soft, staccato swinging.

MUGGING HEAVY : As above, with heavier beat.

WOOD-SHED : To experiment in private with a new song.

KICKING OUT : Very free, enthusiastic improvisation.

SITTING IN : When an outside musician drops in by invitation to play with a swing band or group.

SWINGMAN : A swing musician.

SENDER : A word or phrase that sends a band into swing playing as the phrase: "Swing It, Boys!" or "In the Groove!" or "Let's Mug One for the Folks!" etc.

SWING THAT MUSIC

By HORACE GERLACH
and
LOUIS ARMSTRONG

Swing Tempo

My heart gets a chill ___ I feel such a thrill ___ My feet won't keep still ___ When they

COPYRIGHT 1936 BY LONGMANS, GREEN & CO.

swing that mu - sic a rhy-thm like that _

_ puts me in a trance. _

You can't blame _ me for want-ing to dance _

BENNY GOODMAN—CLARINET

Swing That Music

As Played on the Clarinet

By BENNY GOODMAN

SWING THAT MUSIC

COPYRIGHT 1936 BY LONGMANS, GREEN & CO.

CLARINET

TOMMY DORSEY—TROMBONE

Swing That Music

As Played on the Trombone

By TOMMY DORSEY

SWING THAT MUSIC

COPYRIGHT 1936 BY LONGMANS, GREEN & CO.

JOE VENUTI—VIOLIN

Swing That Music

As Played on the Violin

By JOE VENUTI

SWING THAT MUSIC

COPYRIGHT 1936 BY LONGMANS, GREEN & CO.

VIOLIN

Copyright The Condé Nast Publications, Inc.

LOUIS ARMSTRONG—TRUMPET

Swing That Music

As Played on the Trumpet

By LOUIS ARMSTRONG

SWING THAT MUSIC

COPYRIGHT 1936 BY LONGMANS, GREEN & CO.

TRUMPET

Photograph by Charles Peterson

BUD FREEMAN—TENOR SAX

Swing That Music

As Played on the Tenor Sax

By BUD FREEMAN

SWING THAT MUSIC

COPYRIGHT 1936 BY LONGMANS, GREEN & CO.

TENOR SAX.

Photograph by Charles Peterson

RED NORVO—XYLOPHONE

Swing That Music

As Played on the Xylophone

By RED NORVO

SWING THAT MUSIC

COPYRIGHT 1936 BY LONGMANS, GREEN & CO.

XYLOPHONE

CARL KRESS—GUITAR

S'wing That Music

As Played on the Guitar

By CARL KRESS

SWING THAT MUSIC

COPYRIGHT 1936 BY LONGMANS, GREEN & CO.

GUITAR

STANLEY DENNIS—BASS (STRING)

Swing That Music

As Played on the Bass (String)

By STANLEY DENNIS

SWING THAT MUSIC

COPYRIGHT 1936 BY LONGMANS, GREEN & CO.

RAY BAUDUC—DRUMS

Swing That Music

As Played on the Drums

By RAY BAUDUC

SWING THAT MUSIC

★(A) { Left stick play four beats—(Short press roll on second and fourth beats)
Right stick play as written

★(B) { Left stick play four straight beats
Right stick play as written, with syncopated accent as marked.

COPYRIGHT 1936 BY LONGMANS, GREEN & CO.

DRUMS

*(A) { Short press roll both sticks - Strong accent four beats
Left stick.

CLAUDE HOPKINS—PIANO

Swing That Music

As Played on the Piano

By CLAUDE HOPKINS

SWING THAT MUSIC

PIANO
Swing Tempo

COPYRIGHT 1936 BY LONGMANS, GREEN & CO.

Other DA CAPO titles of interest

THE ART OF JAZZ
Ragtime to Bebop
Edited by Martin Williams
268 pp., illus.
80134-5 $8.95

THE ENCYCLOPEDIA OF JAZZ
Leonard Feather
527 pp., over 200 photos
80214-7 $22.95

THE FACE OF BLACK MUSIC
Photographs by Valerie Wilmer
Introd. by Archie Shepp
120 pp., 110 photos
80039-X $13.95

52nd STREET
The Street of Jazz
Arnold Shaw
378 pp., 64 photos
80068-3 $12.95

FROM SATCHMO TO MILES
Leonard Feather
258 pp., 13 photos
80302-X $10.95

JAZZ: America's Classical Music
Grover Sales
255 pp., 61 photos
80491-3 $13.95

JAZZ MASTERS OF
NEW ORLEANS
Martin Williams
287 pp., 16 pp. of photos
80093-4 $9.95

JAZZ MASTERS OF THE 20s
Richard Hadlock
255 pp., 12 photos
80328-3 $10.95

JAZZ MASTERS OF THE 30s
Rex Stewart
283 pp., 13 photos
80159-0 $9.95

JAZZ MASTERS OF THE 40s
Ira Gitler
298 pp., 14 photos
80224-4 $12.95

LOUIS: The Louis Armstrong
Story 1900-1971
Max Jones and John Chilton
302 pp., 50 photos
80324-0 $10.95

LOUIS ARMSTRONG
Hugues Panassié
149 pp., 32 pp. of photos
80116-7 $7.95

SATCHMO
My Life in New Orleans
Louis Armstrong
220 pp., 20 photos
80276-7 $10.95

UP FROM THE CRADLE OF JAZZ
New Orleans Music Since
World War II
Jason Berry, Jonathan Foose,
Tad Jones
299 pp., 91 photos
80493-X $16.95

Available at your bookstore

OR ORDER DIRECTLY FROM

DA CAPO PRESS, INC.

1-800-321-0050